TELLING TALES

STORYTELLING IN THE FAMILY

TELLING TALES

STORYTELLING IN THE FAMILY

GAIL DE VOS
MERLE HARRIS

WITH AN INTRODUCTION BY CELIA BARKER LOTTRIDGE

ILLUSTRATIONS BY BARBARA HARTMANN

DRAGON HILL

PUBLISHING

Edmonton

Canadian Cataloguing in Publication Data

De Vos, Gail, 1949-
    Telling tales

    Includes bibliographical references.
    ISBN 1-896124-01-1

    1. Storytelling. 2. Family--Folklore. I. Harris, Merle. II. Title.
Z718.3.D4 1995   808.5'43   C95-910749-5

Printed in Canada by Quebecor Jasper Printing, Inc., Edmonton, Alberta

95 96 97 98 99   10 9 8 7 6 5 4 3 2 1

Published in Canada

DRAGON HILL PUBLISHING
5541-39 Avenue
Edmonton, Alberta, Canada
T6L 1B7

DEDICATION

To two of the best storytellers in our family,
Anne and Jack de Vos.
GdV

In memory of my favourite childhood storytellers,
Charlotte Gordon, Jimmy Key and Samson.
MH

TABLE OF CONTENTS

Acknowledgements

When Gary Whyte approached us about writing a book on story-telling for parents, we were delighted. We had both been using story in our family life long before we met each other, and although we come from different backgrounds, our friendship has been cemented through a common bond—story.

Our thanks to fellow storytellers Celia Barker Lottridge from Toronto and Ruth Stotter from California for their support and enthusiasm.

Particular thanks must go to our families for their support, their love, and their permission for us to tell you these tales.

THE STORYTELLING DOLL

The storytelling doll, an expansion of the mother and child figurine, was created by Helen Cordero, of Cochiti, New Mexico. Her first storytelling figure, of a pueblo man with five children in his lap, was crafted in memory of her grandfather in 1964. Since that time the overall image of the storytelling doll has become a symbol for storytelling in the western world.

The doll in this book was created by Barbara Hartmann who had examined many storytelling dolls and was particularly inspired by a doll created by Ramus Suina. The faces in Barbara's doll have a variety of ethnic origins to identify the doll as a universal symbol of the storyteller.

PREFACE

Independently of one another, and in different ways, we have used storytelling as focal points in our lives. We are both professional storytellers who also use storytelling extensively in the raising of our children. Besides telling stories and conducting storytelling workshops, for all ages, in schools, libraries, and festivals across the country, we are resident storytellers at Fort Edmonton Historical Park. Each summer we bring the stories of our community's past alive for visitors to the park. One of the side benefits of this endeavour is the stories that are told to us in return . . . "that reminds me of my. . . ."

Gail teaches storytelling at the university level and specializes in telling stories to junior and senior high school audiences. Merle's focus is telling stories to younger children and their parents.

One aim in this book is to cover all facets of storytelling in the family from traditional nursery rhymes to family histories and all stages of child-parent relationships. The journey we take you on, however, can be one of your own design. Feel free to use your own "itinerary" but, for your ease, we have organized our discussions on storytelling in five sections.

Section One introduces the reader to our stories—how we became storytellers ourselves—and to our conviction on the values and functions of storytelling for members of a family, regardless of age. Section Two consists of three chapters dedicated to recognizing, finding, and developing stories from your family members and yourself. The last chapter in this section, Chapter Five — "Family Lore," is based on feedback from our children on their favourite stories and their rationale for their choices. Gail has two daughters in high school and Merle has two adult sons.

The two chapters of Section Three explore the tools of the storyteller: developing, learning, and telling the tales. Section Four delves into the world of universal tales: the folklore of all cultures. Included in these chapters are discussions on nursery rhymes and their place in modern society and the adaptations of traditional folktales, myths, legends, jokes and riddles in modern novels, movies, television programmes, advertisements and the like.

We have written this book in a conversational tone and, because of this, have chosen not to use footnotes and references in the text but, rather, to dip into our own personal experiences and family stories. To aid those who wish to extend their journey further, we have included several selective resource lists following our discussions.

Gail de Vos and Merle Harris
Edmonton, Alberta
June, 1995

INTRODUCTION

Storytelling, that basic human activity of sharing news and remembering the past, surely began in the family. Sitting around an open fire or the kitchen table, washing clothes in the river or husking corn, family members in all places and in all eras have entertained one another with anecdotes about recent events and old tales handed down from earlier times. The stories told became shared experiences and helped all involved to know who they were and where they came from.

But what about families today? Even the kitchen table may not be a regular gathering place and times spent simply talking together may be few and far between. As you will read further along, there is no doubt that people of all ages still love stories. Jokes, gossip, tabloid "news," and urban legends are passed around with gusto. In libraries and schools children sit entranced as they listen to the storyteller. Books of fairytales, traditional or retold with a modern twist, are reliably popular. Movie versions of old tales and legends abound.

But where is the family in all this? Do we tell the personal stories that will help us understand the people we share our lives with? Do we know the stories of our ancestors, of who they were and how they came to make the choices that brought us together in a certain place to be the family we are? Does each person in the family realize that he or she has stories to tell and that all stories deserve to be listened to, at least once?

Some families, of course, do tell stories and know that they do it. Some even have an "official" family storyteller. For others, it is an unrecognized and possibly undervalued part of their family life. They may even feel that telling stories about themselves is not quite right and prefer to think of themselves as recounting facts. Still others simply don't tell each other of experiences and memories. These families are too busy with the immediate moment or with some form of media which, if it tells stories at all, tells the same stories to everyone.

Families who do not tell stories or who don't value storytelling miss out on a very effective way of knowing each other and their common history. They also miss out on the very valuable experience of being heard by, and of listening to, the most important people in their lives and on the closeness and joy of sharing a story.

One of the great things about family storytelling is that it can be reinvented by each family. There are no rules, only guideposts and suggestions. Gail de Vos and Merle Harris are both experienced storytellers and experienced family members. They have thought about storytelling in their own lives and have identified its significance to them as children, as young adults and as parents. As you read about their experiences you may become aware that there are more stories in your own life than you had thought. You will probably be inspired to turn some of your experiences into stories and to encourage other family members to do the same. The guideposts you will find here will help you in your storymaking. And you may find yourself searching your memory and the memories of any handy grandparents, aunts and uncles for stories of the family's past.

You will find out more about other kinds of stories you might want to tell, including folktales and myths, nursery rhymes and riddles. The truth is that all stories become "ours" if we love them and share them. It is the sharing, the telling and listening, and the common experience that results, that is invaluable. As you follow in the footsteps described in these pages you may well find stories creeping into unexpected corners of your family life to the enrichment and joy of all.

Celia Barker Lottridge
Toronto, Ontario
June, 1995

SECTION ONE
ONCE UPON A TIME

This is what fools people: a man is always a teller of tales, he lives surrounded by his stories and the stories of others, he sees every-thing that happens to him through them; and he tries to live his life as if he were telling a story.

Jean-Paul Sartre

Historians are the custodians of the past; we, the storytellers, are its physicians who strive to keep it alive.

Leon Garfield

ONE

OUR STORIES

Gail's Story

The first story I usually tell to new listeners is the story of how I became a storyteller. It is not, as I assure them, something I had ever thought I wanted to become. I grew up in a small town with one burning desire, to travel and see the world. I left home to attend the University of Alberta and came away four years later a secondary school teacher, a history teacher. My first job was teaching Australian history, nothing I had ever studied, in Australia. An enriching experience, but not as exotic as I had hoped it would be, so I left for Japan. I stopped along the way in Bali, Singapore, Malaysia, Thailand and finally, Laos, where I felt I wanted to stay, and so I did. Several years later, when their civil war was over and all western people were ordered to leave, I returned home to Canada to earn money by working in a stereo store in order to continue on my journey. But fate intervened. As I tell the audience, "a tall blonde guy came into the store, I took one look at him and thought, not bad!" So I got married instead, and after our two daughters were born I returned to university to become a librarian. Because the girls were young I took the first night course available in the faculty—storytelling. I had no concept of what storytelling meant. I was afraid of standing up in front of people and had problems speaking English, the only language I knew, but I thought "*I can do it, I have two small children I can practice on,*" and so I took the course and became hooked on the power of story!

The final assignment in the course was telling a folktale from our own culture. My husband Peter suggested the legend of *The Golem*, a powerful Jewish tale that I researched diligently. I also told it for my first public performance as a storyteller. In the audience that day, a woman started to cry during the telling but she disappeared before I could speak to her. Fortunately, the same woman was in the audience for my next performance. I again told a Jewish folktale, with the same result: the woman sobbed. This time I did manage to speak to her before the day was over. Her story follows mine because since that time we have become fast friends, storytelling partners and co-authors of this book.

Merle's Story

I was that woman. Listening to Gail's telling of *The Golem* and then the story of the *Menorah*, I suddenly realized not only the power of story, but the power of the teller. As a young girl in South Africa, I was friendly with a Jewish girl and treated as an extended family member. Their grandfather was a marvellous storyteller and, over the next few years, I heard him tell *The Golem* and other stories many times. The second story Gail told was about an old man who wanted to surprise his son's family by replicating the menorah used by his family when he was a child. He was terribly frustrated that no matter what he did, his menorah did not look quite right. His young grandson crept into the workroom to discover what it was that was upsetting his grandfather. He accidentally dropped the menorah. When the grandfather discovers it lying dented on the floor, he realizes it was the imperfections of loving use that had been missing. When I heard my friend's grandfather tell the story I knew he was that grandson. He never said he was. I just knew.

These stories had been tucked away in my memory bank until I heard Gail tell them. Hearing them again many years later as an adult had a very powerful effect on me. I suddenly realized they were stories deeply rooted in the Jewish culture, but at the same time they were personal stories to the teller. It showed me how a good teller gets the listener caught up in the story and frees them to make their own interpretation.

I was extremely fortunate to have spent my formative years in a small mining town in what was then called Southern Rhodesia, now Zimbabwe, and to have African children as friends. One of my strongest memories is of the stories their parents always told. They seldom chastised or punished us for our misdeeds, they told us stories. One father, Samson, was a particularly good storyteller with a remarkable command of the English language. He was a great favourite of ours.

I never realized the impression these carefree days listening to his stories had had on me until many years later in a busy shopping mall in Hamilton, Ontario. Our youngest son Scott, then about two-and-a-half, decided he was hot, tired, and going to have a temper tantrum. I stood there not knowing what to do, ready to retaliate with a temper tantrum of my own, when I heard Samson speaking in my head: "*Nkosisane* (little madam), why don't you tell him a story?"

Oblivious to the crowd, I lifted my noisy son, beckoned his older brother to follow, sat them down on one of the benches and inspiration struck. I heard myself say "I'm going to tell you a story of a little man who had a temper tantrum" and I launched into:

> *Once, long, long ago there was a poor miller who wanted the King to think he was very important, so he told the King that his beautiful daughter was able to spin straw into gold. The King was extremely greedy and he demanded that the daughter be brought immediately to his castle.*

The poor girl arrived and the greedy King took her to a room that was filled with straw, gave her a spinning wheel and bobbins, and left her in the room with the words, "If, when I return tomorrow morning, you have not spun this straw into gold, you will die."

The miller's daughter was terrified. She found it difficult enough to spin flax into linen, let alone straw into gold. She couldn't believe what her father had done to her and began to cry. Just then the door opened and a tiny man sidled in.

"Good evening miller's daughter. Why the tears?"

"My father told the king I could spin the straw into gold, but I can not and I will have to die."

"If I spin it for you, what will you give me?" asked the tiny man.

The miller's daughter thought for a minute and cried "Oh, my necklace" and she took it off and gave it to him.

He tucked it in his pocket, sat down at the wheel and began to spin and whirr, spin and whirr, spin and whirr—three times round and a bobbin was full. He spun on through the night and when he slipped out at daybreak, the bobbins were wound with gold.

The King was overjoyed, but being greedy, he took the miller's daughter to a larger room filled with even more straw and threatened her with her life again. She started to weep and once again the tiny man was in the room, "What will you give me this time to spin this straw to gold?"

"My ring," she said and as soon as he had it tucked in his pocket, he began to whirr and spin, whirr and spin, whirr and spin and at daybreak the bobbins were wound with gold.

The King could not believe his good fortune and he thought, "she may be the poor miller's daughter, but no one could bring me more riches." He took the girl to an even larger room filled with straw and promised, "If you spin all this straw into gold by the morning, you will be my Queen."

The little man was there almost before the King had left. "What will you give me if I spin this straw for you?" he questioned.

"I have given you all I have," replied the girl, beginning to cry.

"Tomorrow you will be Queen. Promise me your first born."

"Who knows if I'll be Queen," she thought, "but I know if this is still straw tomorrow, I'll be dead." And so she made her promise.

The little man began to whirr and spin, whirr and spin, whirr and spin with such speed, that the room glowed golden. In the morning, when the King saw all the bobbins wound with gold he asked the miller's daughter for her hand in marriage.

The wedding was a grand affair and the new Queen's dress shimmered with the tiny man's golden thread. A year later when she gave birth to a beautiful daughter she'd long forgotten the tiny man. Suddenly, one day, he appeared in her palace room demanding "Give me what you promised me!"

The Queen tried to tempt him to take her riches instead of her child, but he said "No, I would rather have something living than all the treasures of the world."

The Queen so wept and begged the little man to let her keep her daughter that he softened a little and said, "I will give you three days, and if at the end of them you cannot tell me my name, your child belongs to me."

The Queen never slept a wink that night, thinking of all the names she could. The next morning, swearing her messenger to secrecy, she sent him throughout the land to find the little man's name. She herself questioned everyone.

When the little man arrived, she asked, "Is it Scott, Craig, David?" But to each name he replied, "That is not my name."

That day the Queen asked for all the strangest names and when he returned the next day she asked, "Is it Roast-Ribs, Spindleshanks, Sheepshanks?" Again, to every one he replied, "That is not my name."

The messenger returned early on the third day and told the Queen "As I passed through the woods, I came to a high *hill and near it was a little house. In front of the house burned a fire and around the fire danced a strange little man singing this song*

Today I bake, tomorrow I brew my beer,
The next day I will bring the Queen's child here.
Ah, lucky 'tis that not a soul doth know
That Rumplestiltskin is my name, ho ho!

The Queen was overjoyed and rewarded her messenger. The little man arrived soon after and asked "Now, what is my name?" She answered first "Are you Jack?" "That is not my name," he replied. "Are you Harry?" she asked. "That is not my name," he said.

And then the Queen said, "Perhaps your name is Rumplestiltskin?"

The little man jumped up and down in a rage and screamed, "The devil told you that! The devil told you that!" He stamped his right foot so hard it went right through the floor, then he caught his left foot with both his hands and pulled so hard he split himself in two and the Queen was never again bothered by Rumplestiltskin."

It worked! Scott stopped screaming and writhing, and all three of us were caught up in the magic of story. When I'd finished, a still breathless little boy stammered, "No stamp feet!" and we all laughed.

I had re-discovered the power of story. I had been in control without controlling. What could have been a long drawn-out episode with tempers flaring, turned into a positive, happy experience for all, and, most importantly, I too had calmed down and could see things from a little boy's perspective.

Gail's Story Continues

Like Merle, I told stories to defuse potentially explosive situations with my daughters. And, because I had daughters, I told specific stories to enhance their self-esteem and self-image.

> *Once upon a time, not so very long ago, there was a child, a girl child, who was very much like you. She had long dark hair* [In these stories, the heroine always had long dark hair just like mine], *she was very beautiful* [needless to say], *and she was not too tall* [just right].

Telling stories with my children allowed me the freedom to become the heroine I always thought I should be, given a different time and place. I could "correct" the misconceptions that blonde heroines were better than brunette (except when telling stories to my youngest daughter with her blonde curls). Often the stories were tied to reality and my heroine did not always win battles with honours and valour. But regardless of how she behaved, my heroine helped my daughters and myself connect with each other.

It has been stories, and the telling and listening of them, that has connected us since our first meetings. However you may come to the world of storytelling, we hope it connects you to those you care about as well.

All sorrows can be borne if you put them in a story or tell a story about them.

Isak Dinesen

Two

THE VALUE OF STORIES

S torytelling is still alive and flourishing today. Although we don't think about it, we all tell stories. We tell jokes, relate experiences, give explanations and talk about the things we've done. Whenever we want to say something, anything at all, we put it in story form to help articulate our thoughts, emotions and impressions. Storytelling is not limited to "stage" performances but encompasses our experiences and daily life.

The aim of this chapter is to introduce the many roles story-telling plays in the family. We are *all* storytellers, and we are *all* listeners. Storytelling, used informally, creates bonds, increases listening skills, and fosters communication among family members. It provides quality time together and is useful as a parenting tool. More formal storytelling can take place in a variety of family occasions where it can include family history, folktales or popular culture. Storytelling is contagious and thrives on being passed on.

As parents, both of us find that the stories and the storytelling activity in our families aid all of us in our voyages of discovery.

Although we didn't realise it at the time, we both grew up in families which told and listened to stories.

Merle grew up surrounded by storytellers—her grandmother and her friends, bachelor cousin, mother, step-father, and most importantly the Africans with whom she spent her formative years. Over the years she came to appreciate the fact that she was fortunate to hear stories in their purest form—in the truly oral tradition—told by people who were unable to read or write. Often she couldn't understand the words, but through the storyteller's body language and gesticulations, and her own imagination, she understood the essence of the story.

Gail grew up surrounded by an extended family. Because they were an immigrant family, with no other relatives in Canada, the closeness among the members was especially cherished. The stories they told kept their small family core connected as members moved away from their original homestead. It is these stories that have helped Gail establish her value system and forge her identity.

Story is the natural package for transmitting an experience to others in a form they will be able to easily decode and understand. Humans have always been storytelling animals; telling stories helps us make sense of what is happening around us and within ourselves. As life becomes more and more complicated, in a world that seems almost as inexplicable as when it was viewed by ancient eyes, stories allow us to stop and ponder and catch our breath at the same time as they fill us with release and wonder.

In a recent workshop, a participant said, "Isn't it ironic? You are telling us that we all tell stories to make sense of our lives; yet when little children use their imaginations and tell us those stories, we tell them not to make things up."

Irony indeed. Storytelling is not the transmission of "lies" but rather the uncovering of "truths," allowing the listener to glimpse inside the world of the teller's imagination and memory. Storytelling is the most powerful of educational tools which is why it has been the mainstay of religious leaders throughout history. It is not just the story that is so powerful but the storytelling event itself: the entire experience of actively creating images by listening to word pictures.

Folktales and fairy stories, told originally for adults rather than children, lived not on the pages of books but in the memories and minds of storytellers. Historians and folklorists can trace evidence of storytelling being used both as entertainment and education back five thousand years. Storytelling has long been thought of as a healing force—for both the teller and the listener. Boccaccio, in 1353, wrote a classic collection of one hundred stories based on legend, tall tales and local gossip called *The Decameron*. The premise of the collection is ten young people spending ten days telling each other stories in an attempt to keep the Plague at bay. It was thought, in those ancient times, that listening to stories and laughing constituted strong preventive medicine.

Probably one of the most famous of all storytellers is Scheherazade. According to legend, she lived in the harem of a sultan who, each night, selected a new bride and then had her executed in the morning. Scheherazade was chosen and, not wanting to die, she told the sultan a tantalizing and incomplete story which ended with the promise of more to come. The sultan was in a dilemma—should he kill her or hear the rest of her story? He listened the following night and the next. He was so caught up in the spell of her stories that he needed to hear the end. Scheherazade lived a long and healthy life, and so have her stories, now known as *The Thousand and One Nights* (or *Arabian Nights*).

In the somewhat less risky situation of modern family life, stories can still seem like a survival strategy. They can be used, for instance, to catch the attention of children when they are misbehaving. Telling a story instead of reacting to the behaviour is a sanity saver. It gives you time, while telling, to work through the problem. Falling back on telling a story calms you down and allows you to put the situation into proportion. It is a good idea to have characters with whom your child(ren) can identify, someone with whom they can connect. They listen in order to learn what "their counterpart" is going to do next. If you feel that some form of discipline is needed, you can end by asking "and what do you think should happen now?" Children mete out far harsher punishment than we would ever dream of, and accept it quite readily when it's their idea. At some stage they realize the lessons they learned best were those they worked out for themselves.

For Merle, using stories as a parenting tool, giving her time to calm down and think rationally, became a way of life. She would tell fairy tales, I-remember-when stories, or would make up stories about children, toys or animals. It is amazing what children will take from a story that they won't listen to in a lecture.

Merle found she didn't restrict her stories to her own children. For instance, there was a little boy in their neighbourhood who was a menace. One of his worst traits was throwing sand around when playing in the sandbox and no amount of lecturing and banning him from sandboxes seemed to solve the problem.

> *One day I sat on the edge of the sandbox and told everyone a story about a little boy (almost identical in age and looks to the menace) who loved to throw sand and who couldn't understand why everyone got so upset. The wind, which is always around even when it isn't blowing, had been watching his behaviour for months and decided to play a trick on him. Suddenly, as the boy flung a fistful of sand, a strong gust blew it all back into his wide-open eyes. The problem child was hooked, hanging on to every word, and I confess to getting quite carried away with the consequences and the hospital visit, but I never had problems with him throwing sand again.*

Merle's dad always seemed to know when she had been untruthful—be it a little white lie or a whopper. However, he seldom confronted her outright. He would just quietly recite "*Oh what a tangled web we weave, when first we practice to deceive.*" She would know that he was suspicious and would then find ways of confessing without losing too much face. She learned on those occasions that the guilt one carries, knowing one has done wrong and dreading being discovered, is the real punishment. Being allowed to confront the problem and own up to it teaches far more than being scolded and punished.

She also remembers the story Samson once told to encourage the child involved in petty stealing from the grocery store to come clean:

Once, not too long ago, nor too far away, there was a small village where everyone knew one another and where life was good. Then people started to notice little things were going missing—fewer eggs to be collected when the owners knew the hens were laying well, levels of the maize and millet storage bins going down too rapidly, an occasional kid vanishing from the goat herds. The chief repeatedly asked for the thief to stop stealing or own up to the thefts but the problem continued. He summoned a songoma *(a wise old woman or witchdoctor) to come and help solve the situation. The old crone arrived with only a three-legged cooking pot. She asked that a hut be constructed with a small front and back entrance. While this was being done she sat and questioned the villagers, all the time running her fingers around the rim of the pot. When the hut was complete she went in and placed the pot on the floor of the dark interior. She stood at the entrance, the chief at the exit, and the villagers were asked to walk into the hut one at a time, run their hands around the inside of the pot and walk out. The pot would identify the guilty person. When nearly all the villagers had passed through the hut, the chief stopped a man and declared him guilty. "But the pot didn't speak!" claimed the man. "No," replied the songoma, "your guilt did. Your hands are clean because you didn't touch the pot for fear it would speak. They should be covered with soot."*

Samson allowed the magic of the story to speak for itself. He didn't point out the moral or explain why he told the story. We, too, must trust our children to understand the message in the story and stop ourselves from preaching. We can learn how to do this from the many fairytales in which the wicked are punished and the good are rewarded, without much fanfare or in-depth discussion. Children interpret this treatment as fair.

Children who have become used to listening to stories in their formative years will find listening an invaluable skill in school and university or college. Merle's sons tell their parents that of all the things they taught them over the years, the ability to listen, to concentrate and take in what is being said almost effortlessly, is the most valuable.

When Merle's son Craig was in his first year of university he took an English literature course. The first mid-terms came round as they finished reading the selected short stories, and had just begun *The Great Gatsby* in class, reading from and discussing the first four chapters. Somehow, with all his other classes, he hadn't gotten around to reading the chapters, but he felt sure the exam would concentrate on the short stories. He was in for a rude awakening. Three of the four questions were on *The Great Gatsby*! Close to panic, he completed the short story question and then thought back to the class discussions. He said he got high marks on that exam because all the listening he had been subjected to over the years paid off. Listening to and retaining information had become automatic and although he decided not to rely solely on memory after that, he was grateful he had spent so many years listening.

Time to listen, and time to talk are necessary requirements for a healthy family, as well as for successful students. The families whose members are in constant communication with each other are more likely to remain strong because they are using stories as conduits to discussing problems.

Stories are extremely portable and can be told anywhere and any time. The tellers and listeners carry an entire repertoire in their hearts and imaginations where the stories lie waiting to come out when they are most needed.

These stories most frequently surface during casual conversations, face-to-face or on the telephone. Such anecdotes are told naturally, without thought or advance preparation, in response to a comment or to illustrate a point or explanation. Talking long distance to family members and friends usually involves the sharing of recent, often funny, occurrences that have taken place. The stories are bridges over geographical distances, keeping others informed about what is happening to, and with, family members and friends. These relationships, grounded in the past, are kept alive through the tales related about the present. These stories also shorten the distance on a long journey, help chase fears away in a hospital or doctor's examining room or at bedtime in a strange place; they distract a wiggly baby or bored toddler in a long line up, and connect parent and teenager where nothing else will.

Along with "informal" storytelling situations, family members may participate in more "formal" storytelling activities. These involve the conscious effort of the parent or child teller to tell a particular tale to the audience of choice. These stories, like the more informal ones, are often based on life experiences, family history, remembered tales, and folktales from books. They are told at family celebrations such as weddings, anniversaries and milestone birthday parties. But the thing to remember is that, regardless of the type of story told, the storytelling activity reaps rewards.

Telling stories is linked, in many minds, with certain traditional times, which are, indeed, often very appropriate. Bedtime is the first ideal time that comes to mind. Telling stories after snuggling a child into bed speaks of a calm and caring ending to a day that may have been fraught with activity and emotional imbalances. For both the parent and the child, the story helps to close the day with a meaningful experience. Some people, in fact, equate storytelling and reading to children only with the bedtime routine. When Gail's children were quite young, they asked a new acquaintance to tell them a story. The response, "It's not bedtime yet!" caused confusion in the minds of the two story-hounds. Storytime was *anytime* for them.

Another ideal time for telling and listening to stories is while travelling on holiday trips or even on daily trips to work and school. These tiny capsules of intimate time can be used to start a tradition of telling stories, or better yet, can start a series of related tales about a family member or a character specially created. A character who travels along with the family on their journeys and accompanies them in their travails through the years often voyages with subsequent generations, because your children will tell their children the stories with which they grew up.

Once you have arrived at the end of the journey, there are numerous other opportunities for telling stories. Waiting in the doctor's office? Tell a story. Reached your holiday destination, found the perfect camping spot? Tell a story while you pitch the tent. Arrived at a family reunion? Stories and storytelling are always first on the agenda.

We strongly believe there is no one correct time to tell stories, and, in fact, there are very few times when it is not appropriate. Stories have always been told to pass the time of day while people were busy doing routine chores and this is still a perfect opportunity. Tell a story to keep hands busy and to pass time quickly.

All aspects of story and storytelling are important, but the chief value of telling and listening to stories within the family is that parents and children spend quality time together. Often, the highlight of childhood memories is the time spent listening to the stories of grandparents, other family members and friends. Gail remembers, as a child, listening to and joining in with her dad singing the story of the "rotten" peanut. She also remembers, as a mother, her children listening and joining in with him during their early years. He always prefaced his stories the same way: "When I was a little girl. . . ." After squealing with laughter and delight, the girls would correct him about his gender and then would settle down to listen to whatever he had to say. Gail can hardly wait for the stories about her dad when he was a little girl, and the adventures he had with the "rotten" peanut, to filter down to her grandchildren.

The "story" of the rotten peanut is an old folk song, and has many different versions.

> *Found a peanut, found a peanut,*
> *Found a peanut late last night.*
> *Late last night I found a peanut,*
> *Found a peanut late last night.*

> *Broke it open, broke it open,*
> *Broke it open, late last night.*
> *Late last night I broke it open*
> *Broke it open late last night.*

> *Found it rotten . . .*
> *Ate it anyways . . .*
> *Got a tummy ache . . .*
> *Called the doctor . . .*

Cut me open . . .
Died anyways . . .
Went to heaven . . .

Unfortunately, in these days of mass communication, simple face-to-face communication among family members seems to be at a premium. When was the last time you sat down with your family and listened to one another? In many families, meal time is a rushed event, a time of refueling before additional engagements must be met, and oftentimes the television is competing for attention. There seems to be no time to listen to the words or stories of others.

This is a concern of ours because we realize that in many homes, television is usurping the role of storyteller. Although television is not an ogre, it does need to be viewed in moderation, especially when children are young. Because it is primarily a visual medium, listening skills are dulled by television watching. Television allows the viewer to "tune out"; the images on the screen show enough of the action and one can understand what is happening without the need to really listen, or use the imagination.

We both strongly believed that our children needed only minimum amounts of television watching while they were small, and that because of this they learned to be selective in their programme choices. Merle, having grown up—without adverse effects—in a country that had no television, was perhaps especially conscious of what her sons watched. One of the programmes she felt the boys could survive without watching was the "Dukes of Hazzard." When Craig was in grade three, his teacher called to say he was surprised that Craig had watched the programme the previous night. Merle replied he hadn't, but the teacher was insistent and said he would prove it. An apologetic, but bemused, teacher arrived at their home after school to explain. While on supervision at morning recess he had listened to Craig leading the conversation about the previous night's episode. After talking to Merle, he took Craig aside during afternoon recess and asked him where he'd watched the programme. Craig confessed he'd never seen an episode, but each week he would listen to his friends talking about it. There seemed to be a pattern to these verbal replays, and he found he could join in the discussion and make as much sense as anyone else without even seeing the show.

Televisions, once viewed mainly in the family room, are now becoming commonplace in children's bedrooms. This means television watching is becoming a solitary occupation. Family members, instead of selecting and watching a programme together, isolate themselves from one another to watch the programmes of their choice alone. There are some wonderful programmes for family viewing, but they should not be used to take the place of mouth-to-ear, eye-to-eye, and face-to-face communication—family storytelling.

Oral cultures understand this. An African parable explains the differences between television and the living storyteller.

An enthusiastic television salesman, knowing the importance placed on storytelling in Africa, decided this was a market he should explore. He set off with a number of television sets, and coils and coils of cable. He arrived at the first village to find all the villagers gathered in the village square listening to the village griot *(storyteller). He was delighted at his good fortune to find so captive an audience and quickly set up his equipment on the outskirts of the crowd.*

When everything was ready, he approached the crowd. "I have brought you a new storyteller who is able to tell you many stories."

"We are quite happy with the storyteller we have," the crowd answered. "He, too, knows many stories."

"How many stories do you know?" the salesman asked the griot.

"Many, many stories of my people. I don't know, maybe a few hundred," replied the griot.

"This storyteller knows thousands of stories, each one is new and different. Gather round and listen to them. In a year you will never hear the same story again," he invited the crowd.

One by one the villagers gathered around the television, calling to others to join them until they were all engrossed

*watching the television. Smelling success, the salesman said
he would leave the television with them for a week.*

*As he was leaving, he noticed the storyteller was not
among those watching, and feeling just a little guilty, he
suggested he join the others and be entertained himself. The
old man gently declined.*

*When the salesman returned to the village the following
week, certain he was going to sell many sets, he could again
see the crowd gathered in the square. However, when he got
close up he discovered they were clustered around the
storyteller, who once again held their attention, while the
television set sat dark and mute in the background.*

*"Did you not enjoy the new storyteller's stories?" he
asked.*

"Oh, yes," was the chorus, "they were very good stories."

*"Well, why are you listening to your old storyteller
again?"*

*"It is quite simple," replied one man. "You see, although
the new storyteller knows many stories, he does not know
us."*

While she was living in Laos, Gail saw first hand how quickly the
glamour of television wore off. When the sets first arrived, they
were placed in the open windows of wealthier homes—the screens
towards the community so everyone could share the experience.
However, the community soon tired of the television and moved
to a neighbouring porch where they could listen to each other's
stories.

Television is primarily a one-way communication, whereas
storytelling is, by its very nature, a two-way communication. In a
family, not only should parents tell stories, it is equally important
that children be allowed to tell their stories, and that parents take the
time to really listen. As children grow older, the communication
channel will still be there, open and working, because both sides
have learned how to listen.

By listening to the stories children tell, regardless of their age,
we can learn about them, their thoughts and visions. For children,

both listening to and telling stories can be healing during a time of turmoil. Unfortunately, we are often too busy to take the time to listen to the stories our children are telling us.

Years ago, a consultant with the Hamilton School Board gave Merle these words which were written by a so-called "problem" child. They contain a most eloquent plea which speaks for all children.

If only you would listen,
I'll tell you how I feel
Share my joys, my sorrows,
If only you would hear.

But no, you seldom listen.
Before I've uttered ten short words
You interrupt . . .
You've guessed the rest
And tell it back to me.
Or it reminds you
Of a bigger, better yarn
That you must share—
IMMEDIATELY.

If only you would listen,
Forego your chance to show
How rich your life has been
In happening.
You'd understand the way I feel
With fascinating stories of my own
Fermenting painfully within.

But you would also learn
What makes me laugh,
And cry,
And disagree with you.
My hopes and dreams
Might make our life the richer,

Ideas to spark your soul
And draw you close to me,
If only you would listen.

Often children need time to get their stories out, they can't be hurried. Because what they have to say is important, we need to hold back our advice, and not only listen, but also hear. When we listen to a child's story, it is important for us to sit back and digest what we have heard, rather than to immediately react.

We all want what is best for our children, we want them to grow up filled with compassion, courage and common sense. It is also imperative that we enable our children to have a focus in life, to retain what they hear and, most importantly, to use their imaginations. Telling good stories to your children—and listening to their stories—enriches them in so many ways: they become aware of the magic and importance of words; their imaginations, once stimulated, never fade; and they carry with them a treasury of memories which will have lasting benefits.

SECTION TWO
TELLING TALES: FAMILY STORIES

Telling stories is among the least costly and yet the most effective means of entertainment available to any family.

Anne Pellowski

The web of our life is of a mingled yarn, good and ill together.
William Shakespeare

THREE

EATING WORDS

*F*amily stories are stories involving the members of an extended family and events which may have happened within their living memory or may have been handed down from earlier generations. These stories may tell of a time in which someone did or said something interesting, amusing or just plain dumb. The stories that are related the most often are the ones that amuse the audience (and the teller) as well as those that explain how the family came to exist. Many of these become instant favourites that are retold, embellished and, through this process of retelling, become more polished. Simply telling the story of an event makes that event even more outstanding and eventually more vivid in both the teller's and listener's memory.

Family stories do not have to be polished "pearls of wisdom" but rather can be simple expressions of what took place that particular day. Meal times, in our households, are filled with stories of what happened at school and at work. We listen to each other and, as well, constantly interrupt one another to make comments and observations. Our families are very vocal, relating tidbits that we know interest other family members. These tidbits are always told in story form and naturally, when two members of the family have been to the same event, we often hear two completely different versions. There is no television droning in the background, deflecting attention away from our conversation. Listening to and telling these stories brings the family closer together, helping to create a channel of communication from a very early age. You may not think of this as storytelling but, instead, regard it as gossiping. However, gossip is one form of storytelling. Often the item of gossip does not make any sense to the listener unless it is placed in some sort of context—in the form of a story with a beginning, a middle and an end.

As a result of these informal meal time storytelling sessions, our children have learned to use this format to discuss many of their problems with us, knowing that their point of view will be listened to and respected.

Sometimes the stories and resulting discussions around the dinner table remind us of a similar story or event in our family history. These stories are treasured because we know a grounding in family history establishes a firm footing from which to build and flourish. The stories also provide an understanding of family members who are no longer with us.

While we have always taken this informal family storytelling for granted, we have discovered that it is not a common practice in all families. At a writing workshop this past year, the participants were to discuss some aspects of their family history—tell a story of how the family came to be. We watched the face of one of the participants as she looked bemused, flustered and then confused. "But," she blurted, "my family never told me any of those stories. I don't even know how my parents met—my children do not know how my husband and I met!" She finished the workshop eager to telephone her parents to find out their stories and to have her and her husband tell their children their family tales.

Occasionally it is someone from outside the family who provides a missing link in the story of our family. Merle learned about her father's illness from a stranger:

When I was twenty I attended a banquet with my cousin Bill. During cocktails, I sensed someone staring at me and when we sat down to dinner the feeling persisted although no one seemed to be looking directly at me. Eventually, halfway through the evening, an older gentleman came up to me and asked if my last name was Gordon. When I replied yes, he asked if I was Archie's daughter. Again, I answered yes, and a question of my own, why?

It turned out he had been my father's intern eighteen years earlier when he was being treated for tuberculosis, and seeing me was like seeing a ghost because of my uncanny resemblance to my father. The doctor had lost touch with mum after Archie's death when we moved from Northern to Southern Rhodesia a few years later and had often wondered what had become of us.

The doctor told me my father had volunteered for experimental gold injections to cure his TB. The cure had worked wonderfully, but the unforeseen occurred and the gold dust settled in his arteries, clogging them, and slowly killing him. He had been with my father constantly during his last days and was able to tell me that my father seemed to know his death was imminent. On what was to be his last day, my father had begged to be allowed to go home and spend time with me, saying it would be his last chance to see me. The doctors felt he was responding to treatment and needed to be where they could monitor him, but they allowed my mother to drive him to our house. Because it was raining heavily, she carried me out to the car to visit him briefly. Then she had to return him to the hospital. My father was happy he had been able to see me but was also devastated that no one believed his feeling of death. His breathing became laboured and within a few hours of returning to the hospital he died. This doctor had carried that memory and guilt about it all those years.

A few years ago when swapping family stories, Merle was relating this story to Gail's astonishment and wonder. Gail's father, too, had just recently been given gold injections to cure his arthritis. He also had an adverse reaction and almost died, but fortunately they had discovered the clogging (of his lungs) in time and were able to stop the treatment and further deterioration. Quite a family connection!

Numerous themes are universal in family stories. Most families have stories about heroic action and the heroes in their history—how great-aunt Matilda outfoxed the railroad when they wanted her farm—as well as stories about their favorite family rogues and mischief makers. Memories about practical jokes not only make good stories but also demonstrate a sense of fun and play with one's ancestors. Some stories tell of triumphs and survival over hardships such as the Depression, and the pioneer and early settlement experiences. Others tell of innocents (or fools) and their mistakes, lost fortunes—our family would be rich if only great-uncle George had bought the stock he was offered, it is now worth millions—family feuds, supernatural happenings, courtships and migration stories.

Migration stories in particular are so often shared experiences. Both Merle's and her husband David's ancestors immigrated to South Africa in the mid-1800s and they grew up hearing stories of their families' beginnings in South Africa. Learning the stories of early life in Alberta to tell at Fort Edmonton, Merle is constantly amazed at the similarities between these two countries. Granted the climates and hardships differ, but the grit and determination of those early pioneers was remarkably alike. The Red River carts used by Canadian pioneers bear a strong resemblance to the ox-drawn covered wagons used by the South African *Voortrekkers*. The stories about dismantling the carts and carrying them in pieces over the mountain ranges are nearly identical.

When Merle met David, he was in the process of applying to immigrate to Australia. They had known each other five months before getting engaged and married in three weeks! As she was an only child, she decided that coping with a wedding in a short space of time was enough for her parents and they would explain their plans to immigrate once they were married. About a month later, they had her parents to dinner and dropped the bombshell. Her step-father's reaction was an immediate, "I quite agree with you wanting to leave this country. If we were younger we'd be joining you.

However, if you are going to take our daughter away from us, I want her to go to a country where I know she'll be welcomed. Of all the nationalities I spent time with during World War II, the most decent, generous and honest people were the Canadians and I'll trust them to treat you well. I'd really appreciate it if you considered going there." Needless to say they took his advice, changed their plans, and twenty-two years later they know his advice and their choice of a new home were right.

Gail's in-laws can trace their roots back centuries, documented in historical records in the Netherlands. Her own ancestors came to Canada in the late 1800s to escape persecution in Russia, and did not want to revisit the memories that were so painful for them. Her grandparents were young pioneers to this country, settling in Manitoba and Saskatchewan, and her parents followed in their steps, moving their young family from the familiar to "pioneer" a new life in Alberta. The sense of adventure in the stories of their experiences helps give their children and grandchildren confidence in reaching towards uncharted areas.

When we start reading or exchanging migration stories we find the world is a much smaller, less complicated place than we make it. So many of our problems and achievements share common bonds. For all but the indigenous people of North America, there is a family migration story if you go back far enough. Unfortunately, too often, either because the memories are too painful, or especially today, because we are too busy to listen, an entire era of family history is lost. If you are wondering where to start with your family's stories, sit down with the older generations and start asking questions—stories are waiting to be told, heard and recorded.

Often, family stories are transmitted in fragments, needing time and the stories of several family members to provide the *glue* to produce a logical tale. Sometimes the links between the pieces are never found and need the imagination and vision of the "storyteller" in the family to place them in context.

Some family stories are hidden in other aspects of *family lore*. Family lore includes superstitions, sayings, family meal time and holiday rituals and traditions, songs and family photographs. Stories answer questions about family lore and offer explanations.

How did this belief come to be? Where did you acquire that object and why? Why was that photograph taken? Who took it? Who are all those people in the picture? Often these stories or explanations are taken for granted by members of the immediate or extended family, and are only told when "outsiders" or "newcomers" are invited into the family circle. These sayings and superstitions, therefore, act as a shorthand for the tales and family history.

"Do you want to buy a saw?" Gail's parents ask each other when one of them has said something that is totally out of context in a conversation. They always laugh afterwards and continue on talking. Why ask such a silly question? Gail used to wonder until she heard the story behind it. Apparently, her grandfather had woken up from one of his famous after-dinner naps and startled everyone by interrupting the conversation with "Who wants to buy a saw?" Since no one had been talking about saws, everyone was quite nonplussed until they realized her grandfather was referring to a saw in his dream. After that, whenever any of her family said something totally out of context, "the saw" would be offered for sale.

The importance of these sayings is the common bond all "insiders" experience. Some sayings, like this one, mean nothing without the background story. However, even before Gail understood the reference to the story, she knew the meaning behind the question— someone had just said something really dumb!

Numerous family sayings have developed over time and are now known as proverbs. "Too many cooks spoil the broth," is familiar in many households. In these cases, we do not have to know the stories behind the words: we understand a message that has stood the test of time. Sayings condense the story into manageable segments or "bites" so the entire tale does not have to be told each time.

While Gail was discussing with her parents, immediate family, and her brother Michael, from out of town, types of stories to include in this book, someone asked, "Do you want the meat sandwich?" and everyone roared with laughter except for Michael who did not understand what was funny. Gail's dad started to tell the story but laughed so hard at the memory he couldn't continue. The actual telling was a community effort. As this was the first time they had actually told the story they all had something to add, comments to make, revelations to reveal.

> *Peter and dad were out sailing and got becalmed over lunch. When they finally arrived back at shore my father was abso-lutely starved—he loves his food and needs to eat on time. Mom and I were waiting for them with a platter of egg salad and meat sandwiches. They both consumed the sandwiches as if eating them was an Olympic event until there were only two sandwiches left: one egg and one meat. Dad very gra-ciously asked Peter, "Do you want the meat sandwich?" Peter replied, "No, you can have it." However, the words were barely out of Peter's mouth before Dad snatched up the egg sandwich and devoured it with great gusto, leaving a very bemused audience around the table.*

This is truly a very simple event and perhaps not that significant, but ever since then, all you have to ask, to set anyone in their immediate family into gales of laughter is, "Do you want the meat sandwich?" To make it even more memorable, however, this story-telling event took place the day of Gail's father's last radiation treatment for cancer. He had been in agony for many months, but was finally able to have supper at their house. His obvious enjoy-ment of the memory and of the storytelling with his family is now an integral part of this saying.

This is one of Gail's daughter Esther's favourite stories. It encompasses, for her, the warmth, contentment and family unity they felt that day. After the community telling to Gail's brother, the story will always mean something more to her—it is also a survivor story.

In Merle's family, the mention of "boiled eggs" is enough to have everyone shout with laughter.

> *Mum and her five siblings grew up in relative luxury, the children of a Chief Magistrate in Bethlehem, South Africa. They were waited on hand and foot and Pam, mum's*

youngest sister by five years, never set foot in the kitchen. My grandmother died when mum was thirteen, and when she was twenty, my grandfather married a woman just a few years older than her. By this time only mum and Pam lived at home and they didn't take too kindly to their stepmother. Mum got a job in Durban, many miles and a province away, and Pam insisted on going with her although she was still in high school. Life wasn't very easy for either of them, but mum's years as a Girl Guide stood her in good stead and she could cook basic fare. One day they were offered tickets to a concert and because mum got home from work late, Pam offered to get dinner ready, as long as it was something really simple. They settled on soft-boiled eggs and toast fingers. When mum started climbing the stairs to their apartment she could detect a peculiar smell which got more pungent the closer she got to their door. When she got inside she could hear Pam sobbing, there was lots of steam and a really strong sulphur smell. She rushed into the kitchen and found poor Pam, tears pouring down her cheeks, poking a fork into the rapidly boiling eggs, "Oh, Iris, I don't know what I've done wrong, I've been boiling these eggs for two hours and they're still hard!"

When our publisher, Gary Whyte, read the first draft of this chapter, he was immediately reminded of a saying in his family:

Whenever someone in our family is heading out the door to go skating (with skates in hand), they are asked (in a Scottish accent) "Where are you going?" To which the reply is, "I'm goin' skatin'." The response is "Well, don't forget your skates!" This is immediately followed by laughter and smiles all around.

This is, in essence, a replay of a humourous event from years before. Although the details of the event have long since been forgotten, the saying itself has now been passed on to the third generation of his family.

Other friends were puzzled about family stories until we mentioned meal–time tales. "Oh, that's just like the story of the chicken . . ." and off they went to explain that at every family gathering, this story, plus others, were always told amidst peals of laughter. "Yes," we said, "that's what we mean by family stories."

Mealtime traditions and *holiday rituals* are also part of family lore and are frequently repeated by successive generations without questioning or knowing why the ritual exists. In Peter's family, each meal time re-enacts a tradition that stems from past generations. They consume their meat before they put anything else on their plates. This ritual came about as the result of family ancestors, in the Netherlands, who ate their large meal in the middle of the day. Their home was attached to their place of business, a butcher shop, and they ate what they considered to be the most important part of the meal first, while it was hot, in case they were disturbed by potential customers during the meal hour.

Another of their meal time rituals involves serving mashed potatoes to everyone but Peter, who detests them. He is served "unmashed" potatoes and, whenever there is someone new at the table, he tells them how he has hated mashed potatoes since the time he was served instant potatoes. He hates both the consistency and the look which remind him of paste. This comment is always followed by the story about cornflakes and the time Peter's father was looking after his two older boys for a week. He left for work early each morning, but in consideration of his sons, would get their breakfast ready in advance. This included pouring the milk into the bowl of cornflakes. Since the boys did not eat breakfast for several hours after he left, you can imagine what they faced each morning. Gail does not think any of them eat cornflakes to this day!

Thus one ritual, and the story behind it, becomes a catalyst for another story, and depending on the number of people around the table, another story after that and so on. It does not seem to matter how often these stories are told, the pleasure is in the telling. When Merle heard Peter's stories, the following story was immediately triggered.

My friend Mary hadn't worked outside the home in the twenty-seven years of their marriage and her husband Tom's one demand was that the evening meal be ready on the table when he got home each night. Mary had owned a microwave oven for a few years but only used it for defrosting and heating until she took a course on how to use it. It's strange how things happen, but that one course changed her life. Thanks to her microwave course, she found she needed far less time to prepare the evening meal. She started joining interest groups and taking other courses and still had the meal ready on the table each night when Tom got home. He started objecting to eating anything microwaved. Arguments about whether or not he could tell the difference became the norm. One day she confided to me she knew he couldn't tell the difference because she still occasionally did the main cooking in the microwave, lasagna and casseroles, for example, which she'd finish off under the broiler before serving. Although she could get away with the meat dishes she couldn't with vegetables. When I asked why not, she said because he could see there were no pots or pans on the drying rack. "Why don't you just rinse them and put them in the rack?" Mary thought this was worth trying. It worked and after that she enjoyed her freedom in the afternoons, cooked in her microwave and rinsed her never-used pots and pans.

Hopefully Mary will tell this to her children and grandchildren and they will pass on the story of her spark of rebellion.

Some rituals, with the passage of time, become superstitions. Many deal with the supernatural, many with rites of passage, and some have practical beginnings. Throughout the years, people have used superstitions and the stories behind them to help conquer fears brought on by feelings of insecurity. One superstition known world-wide is that breaking a mirror will bring bad luck. Many cultures tell stories to illustrate how this superstition may have come about.

Long ago, a young Korean farmer was travelling to the big city on business. He asked his wife if there was anything she would like him to bring. "Oh, yes. Please bring me a comb for my hair."

"Good wife, how will I remember, and how shall I choose?"

There was a new moon in the sky that night, a wonderful thin curve of light that reminded her of mother of pearl. "Do you see the moon, good husband? That is the colour and shape of comb I want."

The journey to the city took some days, his business deals kept him very busy for quite a few weeks, and he totally forgot about the comb. The night before he was to return home, he was walking back to his lodgings when he noticed the now full moon in the sky. "Oh, the moon. I'd forgotten I promised my wife I would buy her something shaped like the moon, but what . . .?"

He found a shop and explained to the assistant that his wife had asked him to bring her back an object shaped like the moon, but he could not for the life of him remember what she wanted.

The shopkeeper had just received a shipment of beautiful hand mirrors and said, "These mirrors are round and silver like the moon, and women love to look at themselves in them."

The young farmer had never seen or heard of a mirror, but he bought it and started on his long journey home. By the time he arrived, the moon was beginning to wane, but it still shone brightly when he handed his wife the mirror, proud that he had not forgotten her request.

She, too, had never seen a mirror and when she looked in she found herself gazing at a beautiful young woman.

"How dare you!" she cried. "I ask you to bring me a comb and instead you bring me a beautiful young woman!"

Before he had a chance to respond, his mother-in-law took the mirror and peered in. "Daughter, you are wrong, he has brought back an old and noble woman, perhaps his mother."

"No, she is young and beautiful," cried her daughter.

"Nonsense," her mother replied. "Look again, she has white hair and she is old!"

While they were arguing, the farmer's son came running out eating a rice cake. He looked into the mirror his grandmother was holding and saw a strange boy eating his rice cake.

He shook his fist at the boy and shouted "Give me back my rice cake!" but the thief shook his fist right back, frightening the son and making him cry out.

When the grandfather ran out to see what the commotion was about, his grandson pointed to the mirror and cried out that the thief had stolen his rice cake. The grandfather grabbed the mirror shouting, "I'll catch that thief, how dare he steal from my grandson!" When he looked in the mirror he saw an old man every bit as angry as he was, staring back.

"Old man," he shouted, "how can you look me in the eye when you have stolen my grandson's rice cake? I'll teach you a lesson or two."

He made a fist and punched the thief right in the nose. The force of his punch crashed the mirror to the floor where it broke into a myriad of bits. The family gazed down with wonder at the broken bits of glass with partial images of all of them looking back.

"The next time you want something from the city," exclaimed the frustrated husband, "I think it best if you come with me and do your own shopping. I seem to bring only bad luck."

Merle doesn't remember her grandmother being superstitious but her mother, on the other hand, was incredibly so. She must have told her grandsons some great stories during their short times together because they are well aware of their grandmother's superstitions. If they spill salt, they'll toss a pinch over their shoulders with the remark "There you go, Nan." They tease Merle mercilessly because she has a bottle of seashells collected from different beaches. "Nan wouldn't be too happy about that mum, you know she would not have seashells in the house." (We have no idea why.) At the same time, while claiming not to be superstitious, Merle won't have an all-white flower arrangement in the house. Her mum was fanatical about this, to the extent of stealthily slipping coloured flowers into other people's all-white arrangements to ensure there wouldn't be an unexpected death in that family.

Gail, like Merle, doesn't consider herself superstitious and yet here is how she reacted when she was expecting their first child.

I refused to have baby showers, have the baby's room ready or have the crib brought into the house and assembled until the baby was brought home safely from the hospital. My dad refinished the crib they had first bought to welcome me home as a baby. It remained at my parents' home until Esther was brought home from the hospital. We had thought we would have everything ready for her at that moment. To tell the truth, we were not quite on target. Esther spent her first night in our house snuggled in the laundry basket because of the paint fumes in her room. There were many people confused about my insistence that there be no advance preparation, but there was no confusion from my parents and siblings who, like me, were familiar with my Bobba *(Grandmother) Esther's superstition about newborn babies. How could I ignore her fears and beliefs, even years after she had died, with my first born and her namesake? As proud parents, we took twelve hundred photographs (slight exaggeration) of our new daughter in her make-shift cradle. Each time I see those photographs, I think of my grandmother and of her telling me, as well as passing on to me, her deep rooted superstitions and I know I was right in following my heart. The same thing happened when Taryn was brought home eighteen months later, but since she was sharing the room with her sister, she actually got to sleep in the newly erected crib.*

Merle too had a *thing* about not wanting to be too prepared before their first baby had arrived safely, but she does not remember this as a family superstition. She requested no showers, saying it was sensible to wait and see what sex the baby was, and bought only the real essentials. Luckily, they were loaned a bassinette by their next–door neighbour, and David moved it to their apartment just before he went to bring them home. Nearly two years later, and living in Canada, her next-door neighbour was equally emphatic that she not buy a bassinette or other things before her baby arrived because of the bad luck it would bring. She was delighted when Merle told her she had no intention of doing so.

Family lore, that accumulated treasure trove of family history, is an inheritance that can be shared and enjoyed by everyone. In families, stories are owned by all—there is never any argument about who gets Aunt Maude's most embarrassing moment story, or which grandchild should be told about the day granddad saved the one-room school. Family stories are told for mutual enjoyment, and it is important that each family member retells the stories. These stories are always changed ever so slightly by the next teller. However, even if the facts are slightly altered, the truth of the story is what counts.

*Begin at the beginning," the King said, gravely, "and go on till
you come to the end: then stop.*

Lewis Carroll, Alice in Wonderland

Four

Finding the Story

I f you are wondering where to start looking for family
stories, look first to the subject you are most familiar
with—yourself and what is important to you. The first
two places we suggest you look are in the stories behind your names
and in your "personal timeline"—a chronological outline of important events in your life.

Names identify you all your life and the stories behind them are
very important. Your names are very personal, very much a part of
who you are; understanding why they were chosen helps take ownership. If a child has been named after a relative, for instance, the
child needs to know the reason for this choice as well as the story of
this relative.

Every name has a meaning and when choosing names for your
children it is important you know the attributed meaning. Quite
often names are chosen because they are a reminder of special
people in one's lives, or because they have a pleasant sound. A few
years ago when a group of students was asked to find out the

meanings as well as the stories behind their names, the results gave one mother quite a start. She had chosen Dierdre as a name for her new baby because she like the sound; however, she had not been aware that Deirdre was Celtic for sorrow. The family had, for some time, been having more than their fair share of bad luck and the mother felt that perhaps the name was partly responsible. She decided if they used their daughter's second name instead, they might break the jinx. She had also looked up the meaning of the whole family's given names to reassure herself.

Other stories may have to do with how a person feels about his or her name and what part of their name they choose to use. Even when you may not be aware of why your parents gave you the names they did, you probably know how you feel about your name and why.

The stories of our own names and the names of our children are offered as examples of stories about naming and responses to names. After reading these tales, tell your own by answering these basic questions.

> *Who gave you your name and why?*
> *If you are named after someone, what do you know about that person?*
> *What does your name mean (in baby books)?*
> *Do you like your name? If not, what would you like to be named, and why?*

Gail Arlene is named after two of her great-grandmothers who she never met. Their names were Gittel and Hodel, her Jewish names. Gail's mother, who hates nicknames, translated them into English as simply as possible (Gail and Arlene). Gail, derived from Abigail, means "thy father's joy," which Gail often felt was entirely appropriate while growing up, as she was the only daughter of a man raised in a family of boys. However, there were times when she felt it too common and she wished for a way to change it, enhance it, or shorten it. This did come about—but not exactly the way she had envisioned. It did not dawn on her parents that nicknames can arise from initials, although it should have, because Gail often heard the story from her dad about his brother, the only one with a middle name. Gail's family name is Shukster and her uncle only used his middle initial once because when he wrote it down he realized what it spelled. His name is Albert Solomon Shukster! Gail remembers teasing her brother wherever they went, that her name was in lights (G.A.S.)—at every gas station at least. She also remembers getting yelled at for writing on the outside wall of their new house which was under construction. Her parents do assure her they apologized when they realized the gas lines went right through that part of the wall. Gail's husband Peter uses his second name and has always insisted on it; when he was being taught to say his name he would just gloss over his first name and say, "Petey de Vos." No one ever called him by his first name after that. He doesn't answer to Petey anymore either.

The story of first names is a very important one in Gail's mother's family. Her Bobba Esther was not welcomed by her prospective mother-in-law for many reasons, but one of the major ones was her name. Esther was also the mother-in-law's name and she was concerned—because of a Jewish tradition in which children, and grandchildren, should not be named after a relative who is still alive—that if one of her sons married an Esther, the children from that marriage could never be named after herself. Since the young Esther's sister was already married to the oldest son in the family, it meant not one of her grandchildren could carry her name. This was a very important issue in her life. So important, as a matter of fact, that she had erected barriers to her son's wedding for several years before it actually took place.

Her paternal grandmother also had a concern about her name. When she arrived in Canada as a young girl she took the name Freida which was a close approximation to her Jewish name, Freidl. In her later years she told Gail how she had always detested her English name and wished she had used the literal translation, Joy, instead. She asked that if Gail ever had the occasion to name a daughter after her, could she please use the English equivalent. Gail and Peter's daughters' names, therefore, reflect their family roots. Esther grew up with stories of the Biblical Esther and stories of her great-grandmother Esther for whom she was named. She identified with both her ancient traditional history and with her immediate family member, linking generations together through her name. Esther has three names after three of Gail's grandparents—Esther after one beloved grandmother; Rachel after Gail's grandfather Roy; and Joy, after her dad's mother.

Esther is very proud of all three names and insists that any official correspondence include them all. This is a particularly vexing problem with modern record keeping generated by computers having only two fields for individual's given names.

> *When Esther was very young, she informed the family that everyone would have to listen to her and her father, Peter, because both of them are in the Bible. Taryn and Gail just didn't seem to be as important!*

Taryn Laine, Esther's sister, also knew the history behind her names from an early age and could identify with her Dutch ancestry, and her great-grandmother and great-uncle on that side. The early identification with their name "givers" and the stories that they heard about them from other family members gave them a firm grounding in who they are.

Unlike Gail's daughter Esther, Merle has only one given name. In Durban, newborns weren't allowed to leave the hospital until their name had been registered and the form presented to the head nurse. When Merle's father arrived to take her and her mother home he had forgotten to register Merle and had to rush down to the Registry before it closed or pay another day's stay. Her mother wrote "Merle" on his hand so he would spell it correctly, but when he arrived at the office, with minutes to spare, he couldn't remember the name he had chosen for her—Dawn. Merle has often wondered what he would have done if her mother hadn't written her choice on his hand!

She learned the meaning of her name when she was about six and her teacher had scolded her for talking too much. Her stepfather explained that because Merle was French for blackbird, she could tell her teacher she was merely living up to her name. Having only one first name often resulted in her having to recite "Merle Nothing Gordon" to bureaucrats. If she didn't, the person filling out the form would fill in the first two blanks and wait impatiently for her to give them her last name.

When Merle and David were choosing names during her first pregnancy, they wanted a first name that wouldn't be shortened. They chose Craig (stony hill or crag dweller) because it reflected their Scottish heritage, and David (beloved) for continuity. When Craig's brother arrived, they chose Scott (short and Scottish) and Gordon (rounded hill) to keep Merle's family name alive. They think they chose wisely because their sons have turned out to be as firmly rooted and dependable as those hills.

Given names have been around a long, long time. Adam, in the Garden of Eden, named himself and all the animals. The use of family or surnames, however, can only be traced back to the mid–1400s (in Europe, at least) when nobility started using them and they were known as "sir names." Many family names were taken either from the relationship to the man of the house, his occupation, or where the family lived.

Learning the story of where your family names come from is a fascinating undertaking. In the Netherlands, surnames were thought of as a joke when first introduced and many times families took any name they fancied. In the northern provinces, they chose more realistic names—animals, places, occupations—such as de Vos which means the fox. In the south the names chosen were more fanciful. For example Gail's mother-in-law's maiden name was *Varkervisser* (pig fisher), which could have come from the dolphins in the area. Gail's in-laws often tell stories of surnames from that region which are too impolite for publication.

The Harris family name traces its roots back to Scotland where the family was involved in the tweed weaving trade. Entries in the Registration of Births, Deaths and Marriages (Scotland) Act give professions of dyer's finisher, dyer's folder, factory weaver and powerloom tenter.

Another practical and highly recommended suggestion for developing family stories is to make a personal timeline of the major events in your life. Start with your day of birth and any stories you may have heard about it. Gail knew from an early age she was a very clever child: born just one day before Mother's Day and she even managed to get her mom a card, which her mother still has! But even better is the tale of how her father (and the hospital) got her gender wrong.

Her dad particularly loves to tell this tale about Gail being a girl-boy-girl. The story follows the same pattern each time it is retold, with Gail's mother chiming in to fill in details her husband could not know (at the time). In the good old days, of course, when Gail was born, fathers were not allowed in the delivery room.

> Approximately 2:30 in the morning, my dad's aunt picked up the ringing telephone and, after listening intently, woke my dad to tell him that he was the proud father of a girl. (My parents at this time were living in the same house as their aunt and uncle.) My dad says that he had images in his mind of a little girl dressed in dresses. When he phoned his mother, her first reaction was to say, "All that and only a girl!" (My mother had gone through a series of false labour pains.) When my paternal grandmother telephoned the hospital, however, she was told that mother and son were doing fine. She immediately telephoned my father who "took the dress off and put pants on" the child in his imagination. (An important note is that Dad never forgets to mention these images in the retelling of the story—these are very strong memories.) He phoned all the relatives with the news. Everyone who knew my great-aunt was not a bit surprised that she had got the message wrong. After all, it was the middle of the night.
>
> My dad then did the next responsible thing. He telephoned his brother Leonard who had the only other grandchild at the time—a daughter—and said, "I have a son. Ha! Ha!" Even though my father, who comes from a family of boys, wanted a daughter—it seemed the right thing to say.

Dad went to visit my mother during visiting hours, the only time he could be there according to hospital rules, and asked, "How's our son?" This question took mom completely by surprise as she had just finished unwrapping me to do a complete inspection and inventory. "She's definitely a girl!"

When dad got home he telephoned my maternal grandmother who said, "I knew it was a girl all the time." Dad then telephoned everyone else to say that they should ignore the second message, the baby was indeed a female.

A little while later, uncle Leonard and aunt Norma drove by the house. They stopped the car, honked the horn until my dad came out, then they opened the car window, shouted "Ha! Ha!" and drove off.

This is the point where Gail's mother takes up the narrative by explaining what happened in the hospital to her and her roommate. Gail continues:

Their two babies had been born within minutes of each other. When the other woman's husband asked about his daughter, he was equally nonplussed to hear he had a son. "It can't be," he shouted at her. "I phoned the hospital, they told me it was a girl and then I sent telegrams to all the relations in the States. And now you tell me I was wrong!" When he calmed down, he sent new telegrams announcing the birth of his son.

After visiting hours and with the various comedies of errors that had played out in that room, the two new mothers became concerned. They called the nurse who, after bringing them their charts, showed that the nurse who was on duty had indeed put an "M" on my chart and an "F" on the other one. Mom immediately called for her doctor. I didn't look like any one in the family! He said there was no mistake. He had put the band on me himself directly after delivery and since the other woman did not have the same doctor, there was no possible way for the babies to be mixed up. I, the girl, was theirs.

Gail's dad was teased about this for years. Leonard and Norma had been on their way to a party with many of the relatives when they stopped by the house to laugh at his "mistake"—they told everyone the story—and whenever people would see Gail's dad they would ask him things like, "How do you tell the difference between girls and boys?" or "Do girls wear pink booties?" (This is particularly applicable to her father, who is colour blind and cannot "recognize" pink or blue.)

This is a tale Gail heard many times as she grew up, and it is a tale her parents continue to tell their grandchildren. This story, for Gail, opened a window to the way her father thought and, as his "precious" only daughter, helped to shape her.

Other important dates include the first day of school. Gail went to kindergarten in Winnipeg and remembers some of the stories and memories of that time. But grade one will always stand out in her mind because, in less than two months, she attended three different schools, in two different provinces, with a wild and wicked train trip between them (a story which is still told today to demonstrate how mean she was to her younger brother, and which is included elsewhere in this book.)

We have included examples of our own time lines to demonstrate what types of things we hold "sacred." These may not seem important to someone else but do help explain where stories can be found. Because of space restraints we have concentrated on particular times of our lives.

MERLE'S TIMELINE

This extract starts when I was four and ends the year I turned eleven. My childhood was wonderfully free and serendipitous and our sons loved hearing my childhood stories. Now I use incidents from this period in telling stories to elementary school children and when explaining how to make a story quilt: a picture record of events in their lives.

- train journey to Luanshya, Northern Rhodesia (now Zambia)
- mum's wedding, new father, eating banana leaves
- rafting on grey, greasy Limpopo River
- short term surrogates to lion cub
- hit with axe for not sharing tricycle plus my revenge
- move to Southern Rhodesia (now Zimbabwe), Umtali briefly
- then to Penhalonga—Utopia
- the outhouse and the snake deterrent
- Mickey my corgi/cairn–cross dog and CAT
- 8-year differential in girls ages, with me in between
- African friends and their influence
- polio scare—visits to friends in iron lungs
- fractured skull and hummingbirds in my bedroom
- post-Easter flood, stranded across river away from home for 10 days
- talking to the Queen Mother and having my photograph of Princess Margaret appear in Rhodesian newspapers
- the grass snake episode
- introduced to horse riding—mad about it
- Mrs. Alexander and the *Voortrekker* episodes
- "Water, Friend and Foe" essay contest
- start boarding school in Umtali at 10
- Margot Fonteyn's ballet slippers and Sharon's death
- move to Muriel Mine—long train journey for holidays

Although I enjoy telling all of these memories in story form, the reaction of my audiences proves that the grass snake episode is a favourite.

> *Once upon a time I lived on a gold mine in the hills of Rhodesia. There were many poisonous snakes, as well as many harmless ones, but I was scared of all of them. My father decided I needed to overcome this fear and, against my mother's pleas, caught me a grass snake. The snake,*

Slither, lived in a glass box in my bedroom and I learned a lot about snakes. Its body was warm and smooth, not cold and slimy as I had imagined, and I watched fascinated as it shed its skin and I had two snakes! I discovered that snakes feared humans and would slither away when they felt vibrations, so it was a good idea to walk heavily and make a noise when out in the bush.

One afternoon, when I got home from school and went to check on Slither, I discovered that the top of his box had not been secured, and Slither was gone. My father was home and when he heard the news he decided it would not be a good idea to let my mum know the snake was missing. However, we told Solomon, our servant, and for the next few days the three of us kept our eyes open looking for Slither, taking care not to let mum know what we were doing. When there was no sign of the snake, we decided it had escaped outside.

About a week later we were going visiting, and mum went into her bedroom to change. There was a loud scream and a thump! Solomon and I raced into the room to find mum fainted on the floor, with the bottom drawer of her dresser open. In it was Slither and lots of tiny snakes! She'd found somewhere safe to have her babies!

Solomon took charge, gathering up all the snakes and setting them free before running to call a neighbour. Mum recovered. The atmosphere was icy for a while and dad and I never mentioned having a snake as a pet again.

Gail's Timeline

Because my audiences are often students in junior and senior high school, I tell them of my experiences after graduating from school and before marriage. Some of these episodes seem very exotic to my listeners—I tell them so as to exemplify how experiences help to shape our future (even if we don't realize it at the time.)

- graduate from Grade 12
- leave home for University and do not come back as my parents follow me to Edmonton two years later
- University of Alberta; living in residence for two years
- summer job in Red Deer and feeling independent
- moving back home and becoming a family member again
- selling records and stereo equipment to help with university costs
- one friend gets married—spend some time with groom's younger brother (when I return to Canada I marry him)
- graduate from University as teacher
- another friend's dream to go to Australia becomes mine as well; she gets pregnant and stays in Canada—I go alone
- trip to Australia
- discover that teachers in school staff rooms do not communicate with each other —becomes my personal quest—I succeed in getting them talking
- Halloween—not an Australian tradition!
- Christmas in the hottest season of the year
- travelling by motorcycle—up very steep hills
- hitchhiking around Australia
- Melbourne—spend all day in public library doing research on Rasputin after seeing movie *Nicholas and Alexandra*
- Tasmania—radio bulletins telling people to offer rides to hitchhikers; staying in gravel quarry
- decision to go to Japan to teach English as a second language. Because people can stop along the route when flying, arrange to stop in Indonesia, Singapore, Malaysia, Thailand, Laos—never reach Japan!
- "hippy" with magic passport—Canadian and a teacher— opens doors everywhere
- spend several months on the journey (with numerous adventures) but when arrive in Laos, fall in love with the people and stay as long as possible

- Laos (an entire book could be written about this time of my life)
- civil war over—Westerners no longer welcome
- need to leave Laos, arrive Bangkok with help of the American consulate and "No way Murphy"; stay for a month
- fly to Los Angeles with friend Linda, stay with her family for a month and then travel by bus to Canada—kept secret from my parents!
- Linda returns to LA and I need to earn money again—looking for more adventures!
- working at the record and stereo store again—tall blonde guy enters my life

Timelines offer us potential starting points for stories. Obviously, some of the points are filled with tales bursting to be told while others are not as promising. It is not until you complete an exercise such as this that you realize how much drama your life contains.

A common response we have received after telling stories is that we had such interesting lives as we were growing up. "Nothing has ever happened to me so what can I tell stories about?" Our answer is always the same: "Yes, Merle grew up in another country in "romantic" circumstances but Gail's entire schooling (with the exception of the first two months of grade one) took place in one school, in one town, in the middle of Alberta." Gail's growing years were unexceptional. But she does have a good imagination to embellish some of the memories that are most evocative. Her brothers and parents have made the comment that she must have been brought up in another family—they don't always recognize the people, places and activities she tells about in her stories. The truth of the story is always there—but as she polishes the tales and weaves in the suggestions from others, the tales take a life of their own and she doesn't try to stop them at all. Even the stories of her various journeys, steeped in drama, are shaped and changed through numerous retellings and the awareness of reactions of the listeners. Some stories are still waiting to be told.

We do not assume that all memories and stories will be instantly available when you start looking for them. Janet Lunn, a much loved Canadian author, talks of memory as an over-filled closet which, when opened, spills out all its contents. Each time we pack them all back in, we end up with assorted odds and ends that just won't fit, and then we remember.

Opening that closet is triggered by many things: a smell, a sound, a name from the past, a photograph, an object in a second-hand store window. Some memories are happy and others painful. They come unconsciously, and often at times when we are at our most vulnerable. As a result we are selective in what we remember, screening out contradictions, under- or over-emphasizing hardships and difficulties. While we remember bristling at our parents' stories of "When I was young, there was snow to the top of the fences and I still walked five miles to and from school and got all my chores done," we too are guilty of "inflicting" our childhood memories on our children.

Remembering is healthy and necessary. Our lives are an ongoing dramatic experience, and we are shaped by decisions we have made, friendships we have formed or broken, and by family, neighbours and community. Who we are now is the result of years and years of layered experiences.

Other starting points for family stories are physical memories—objects that have been saved and handed down from one generation to the next. *Special family artifacts and photographs* contain stories that are related only when someone asks about the particular item. The question "Where did you get that?" is usually answered by a story. The paintings on the wall, the items on display around the home, the decorations on the Christmas tree, and the dishes we use to serve food, often contain stories. At times the stories may seem mundane but the simple fact of telling the story is the important thing. Again, we find one story is usually the catalyst for many more. "Oh did you do that too? Well, when we. . . ."

Sharing these stories helps to establish an identification with other family members who are sometimes distanced by time and space. Stories of old photographs and artifacts help to formulate an identification and bonding with family members in the past. These stories, once passed on to members of the present generation, can also be told to future generations thus allowing for the continuum of family history. Paintings of Peter's great-grandparents hang on his and Gail's living room walls. In these paintings similarities to Peter's father, Peter's brothers and, depending on the day, their youngest daughter can be seen. Ironically, although Peter is named after both of these people, he does not resemble them but takes after his mother's side of the family.

Because of the way Gail's immediate ancestors came to this country, they have no pictures, objects or stories from that time. The objects and photographs they hold so dear are those of the Canadian branch of the family.

Photographs are excellent catalysts for family stories. When we look at our parents' early photograph albums, we are intrigued by the images of people we know and those we don't, as well as places that our parents used to visit. Who are these people? That can't be auntie, look how young she is there! Why were you so dressed up? These questions require answers and the answers always come in the form of a story. One story will remind the teller of related instances and soon countless tales and snippets of memory are brought to light. Since photographs are not a random sampling of our past but rather a series of selected frozen images, they also tell the story of impressions of ourselves.

In Gail's living room sits a small discoloured ivory frame with a photograph of a chubby, unhappy two-year old holding his backside. She first fell in love with this picture of her father when it sat on her grandmother's shelf. Her Bobba Frieda guarded it very carefully as Gail's father had tried many times to destroy this studio portrait of himself. He had not wanted to sit still and so received a slap on his bottom—forever remembered by his well-placed hand and pouting face. He resented this reminder of his behaviour (and consequences) until he, himself, became a father. After hearing the story of her father's escapade that day—which always led to other stories about his behaviour—Gail discovered a boy and followed his adventures into manhood. The father she knew became more dimensional to her, a fuller character! Her grandmother gave her the photograph because she knew Gail would cherish it—and the stories—as much as she did.

While the boys were growing up, as well as mailing off loose photographs, Merle would make brightly coloured construction paper booklets of various occasions such as birthdays, Christmas, camping trips, or just everyday happenings, for both sets of grandparents. She had great fun laying out the photographs in chronological order and adding captions or stories, together with appropriate newspaper clippings, and pressed flowers and leaves which she knew would be foreign to them. As the boys grew older, she would sit down with them, the photographs and the tape recorder to get their impressions of where they'd been and what they'd done. She'd make up the booklets with their stories and memories as captions to the photographs, and send them off together with the tapes. Later still, they wrote their own captions and stories.

When they visited her mum in 1981, they had a wonderful time looking at these almost forgotten booklets and remembering how it had all been. She got some of the booklets back, and when she came across them last Christmas, the family sat and reminisced. David and Merle were amazed at the boys' memories of various events. They could remember so many things that weren't included in the booklets or the photographs. Mum and dad were also amused at the boys' horror that they had been dressed in matching outfits, quite forgetting that they had chosen the fabric!

Merle's family album is an assortment of boxes full of photographs dating back to their South African childhoods. (The albums are purchased but still empty.) When they look through them now they realize how often we tend to underestimate the importance of "little" happenings at the time. When a family member says "Do you remember . . ." it's amazing how vividly the stories come back despite the fact that many photographs are undated and uncaptioned. She also realizes how quickly time passes by.

One photograph Merle has is of her stepfather in army uniform with a long knitted scarf wound around him. When, as a little girl, she questioned him about the scarf, he told her an Italian woman had taught him how to knit while he was recuperating in her home during the war. When he got back to the front lines he found that knitting calmed him down, and so whenever he could, he would find a quiet spot and knit and knit. He ended up with a few yards of scarf and, he said, some peace of mind. The scarf, however, had not come home with him but remained in Italy, cocooning a fellow soldier in his rough grave, in place of a coffin.

Some evenings, when the family is all at home, turn off the radio and television and bring out those photograph albums. If possible have grandparents, aunts and uncles around and introduce your children, through the photographs, to their distant relatives. Who knows, maybe your four year-old, when seeing your wedding album for the first time, will react the way Craig did. "Oh, that's daddy all dressed up," he said excitedly, recognizing his father instantly. "That's right," Merle replied, "who is that with him?" After studying picture after picture, he shut the album with an I-couldn't-care-less, "Some other lady!"

I am always at a loss to know how much to believe of my own stories.

Washington Irving

FIVE

FAMILY LORE

F amily stories give children not only a sense of identity, but also a connection to their heritage. Children love to hear stories of their parents when they were young. What we did and how we behaved are of particular interest. It is important that our children know that, like them, we misbehaved, made mistakes, and got scolded and grounded. Face-to-face communication, telling our stories *and* listening to their stories, allows children to realize that making a mistake is not the end of the world. These stories of our childhood show us in another light, rather than as adults who seemingly know all the answers. They do get to know us warts and all.

Gail's daughters love the story about her pushing their uncle Ivan off the garage roof. In typical "Charlie Brown and Lucy" fashion, she continually betrayed her brother's reluctant trust in his older sister. "Ivan, I promise, I won't push you off this time!" Famous last words which have been often repeated through the years. They also love the stories told by their father of his temper tantrums. This series of stories are now related *by Gail* after Peter becomes disenchanted with his daughters' displays of temper. They also ask for the story about how Gail and Peter first met, their first date, and they particularly relish these stories told from their grand-parents' point of view!

In Gail's household many brief stories are told about "the man who jumped in the window" and caused disorder in their house. This "man" was created, in frustration, by Peter after numerous claims by all members of the family that they didn't leave the mud on the floor by their shoes, or leave the greasy fingerprints on the fridge, and so on. This "man" has been part of their family folklore for over a decade and is now part of their family history. Every time Gail's parents hear about this "man," they tell how, when Gail was young, she used to blame her grandfather for everything she did—especially for wetting her bed!

As children get older, the stories take on an additional function. Taryn tells her friends the stories her parents have told her about themselves at her age. Her friends are envious of the "cool" parents she has and wish their parents were like them. Her friends' parents probably are but have just not communicated themselves to their children through stories. Because of these stories, which do not always show them in a good light, Gail and Peter have become, and have remained throughout their daughters' teenage years, human and approachable. Gail was not aware that Taryn shared these tales with her friends until we started writing this section and Gail asked her about her favourite "parent" stories. Taryn's insight into the importance of family stories and the reasons for her favourites are quite sophisticated. She loves the stories of Gail taking her younger brother, Michael, with her on dates when she was in university. She appreciates the rationalization behind the practice (he was more fun than some of Gail's dates) but responds, in part, to the fact that these stories are about someone who is closer to her age. (Michael is eleven years younger than Gail.) Several stories appeal to her because of the funny images they conjure.

A favourite story for both Taryn and Esther involves their father when he was much, much younger.

Peter's older brothers were babysitting one Saturday night and, true to their habit, put Peter to bed and turned on the television. They were deeply involved in their favourite program, "The Twilight Zone," with only the light from the black-and-white set flickering in the dark house. Suddenly, out of this dark, they could hear someone coming towards them—moving slowly, steadily, heavily—like a zombie! Terrified, the two boys clung to each other and stared in horror as the creature came closer and closer to the living room where they sat. They listened in amazement as the footsteps turned down the hall, stopping in front of the shoe cupboard. They could hear the cupboard lid being carefully lifted, and then—the sound of someone "peeing" all over the family's Sunday shoes their mother had just polished before going out that evening.

Peter, the "zombie," did not often sleepwalk but his family never let him forget this instance at all. His daughters roll on the floor with shrieks of delight every time the story is told or referred to in conversation.

Stories about former pets are cherished because Taryn is an animal person herself. The stories of Gail's family's experiences with Filonia, a spider-monkey who had no bladder control but had the run of the basement, amaze her and her friends. Because the monkey was a childhood pet, the story also gives Taryn an insight into her own grandparents and her uncles when they were younger.

Filonia was originally a babysitting job for my brother Ivan. One of his teachers had gone away for Christmas break and we moved the monkey to our home for the duration. When the teacher returned, he was accompanied by a new wife and family—and no desire for Filonia's reinstatement. So we kept her. She delighted us and the neighbourhood—jumping off the ceiling to land, with her cold feet, on our unsuspecting shoulders and then cuddling up in our pyjama sleeves while we read a book or watched TV.

Mom's favourite game was connected to Filonia's greedy response to food. Mom would offer her a Cheerio—a large doughnut to a spider monkey—and then another. Filonia would shift the first one to her other "hand" and reach for the second one. When she was offered a third Cheerio the fun would start. Carefully inspecting both hands, she would throw one piece of cereal over her shoulder, transfer the other to the now empty hand and reach for the third. This cycle would continue as long as the cereal was offered to her!

Esther has different favourites. She loves the story of Gail's mother and how her heart stopped every time there was work to be done. Bobba Esther spoiled her daughter—Gail's mom learned very early in life that all she had to do to get out of chores was to stagger to wherever her mother was, state in a quivering voice that her heart had stopped, and sit down and wait. Her mother would pretend to be distressed, get her a glass of water and tell her to sit there quietly until her heart started to work again. An amazing coincidence always occurred—Gail's mom's heart would start beating at the same moment the work was finished! Esther realizes that, because Gail also grew up with this story, she had to be even more inventive than her mother and that, between the two of them, they can recognize any excuse a mile away!

The two early stories about Gail's relationship with her brother Ivan—the garage roof and the train episode (told in Chapter 6)—are favourites because, as Esther says, they show how manipulative Gail has been from day one! Gail thinks it is also because Esther is the older sibling and can recognize the rationale for some of her mother's early behaviour. For this same reason, Esther greatly appreciates the story of her father's babysitting tradition. Minutes after his parents would leave him in charge of his younger brother, Peter would turn all the clocks in the house ahead and inform Bill that it was bedtime. According to Peter, this practice always worked like a charm.

As the girls have grown, Gail's father-in-law has begun to tell them stories of courting their grandmother. They feel honoured by these stories and the trust and openness he is showing them. Their father (and grandfathers) tell them about some of their experiences and "how guys think." Some of these tales are very familiar: Gail's dad told them to her when she was their age. Children enjoy these stories about their parents and grandparents as long as they are entertaining tales and not moralizing. Both girls have assured Gail how important all these stories have been to them as they have matured. These stories have helped to keep the communication channel open through the years of adolescence and, as a parent, she can not think of a more exquisite benefit.

The stories have also provided Gail with possible blueprints for parenting skills and the development of bonds between siblings. She remembers what it was like to grow up as the bossy older sister (and if she doesn't, her parents—and now her daughters—are quick to remind her.) Gail is fortunate to have been surrounded by her extended family most of her life and is quick to acknowledge the important role her family and their stories have played.

Merle, on the other hand, grew up as an only child, living in a community comprised of large families. Although her childhood was exceptionally happy, she always longed for a brother or sister. Thankfully David, who had two brothers and knew what it was like to be a sibling, was able to help her understand that brothers resorting to blows was also part of a happy childhood. When David told stories of how he and his siblings had played and fought together, it put their sons' behaviour in perspective for Merle and got her through many a rough patch.

One night after she had been complaining about the boys' bedrooms being messy, David told this bedtime story.

> *From the time I can remember, I was fascinated by model airplanes and built and flew them.* (He still does.) *As there wasn't enough room in the house for me to set up a work-bench and leave the planes in stages as I made them, I asked dad to get me a piece of plywood which would fit on my bed with room for me to sit and build my planes, and spread things out a bit. There wasn't anywhere else to put it, so when it was time to go to sleep, I would push my "work-bench" down to the foot of the bed, very carefully slide in*

*underneath the sheets and try not to move a muscle while
falling asleep. I slept like that for years.*

The boys particularly loved that story because Merle then stopped
nagging them about untidy rooms!

When they were young, Craig and Scott had four visits with
Merle's mother, and loved to hear stories of Merle's childhood, as
well as stories of their grandmother's childhood and of daily life in
South Africa. The stories they loved the best were, naturally, the
ones where Merle was disobedient. Their favourite tells of the time
when she was five and, together with some older children, went out
into the middle of the Limpopo River at a spot close to where an
African woman had been taken by a crocodile. Merle's stepfather
was so relieved to see her unharmed, he first gave her a few well-
aimed wallops with a slat from a fruit box and then hugged her like
crazy. For quite a while after hearing that story, if they were caught
misbehaving, they would say "But, mum, we don't do *dangerous*
things." They also spent time with their paternal grandmother on
two visits back to South Africa. They heard stories of their dad at
their age and his escapades with his brothers, and had the plywood
"blanket" story verified.

The stories they told their boys were of lives spent in a very
different world. The seasons were changed around—when it was
winter here, it was summer there. Merle spent five years living in a
home without electricity or running water. They were also fascinated
by her stories of life in boarding school.

One of their favourite stories of their beginnings in Canada is of
their first winter here and their first experience with snow. It started
to snow quite unexpectedly one day, and Merle took Craig out to
catch snowflakes on their tongues and watch the green world turn
slowly white. Merle was so excited she phoned David at work to tell
him to go outside immediately. The secretary could not understand
what she was saying, thought something terrible had happened, and
called him out of an important meeting. For the longest time,
whenever David's boss saw the boys, he would tell them about their
strange mother who interrupted a meeting to ask their dad to go
outside and stand in a "snow flurry"!

A few years ago, David went back to South Africa for his parents' fiftieth wedding anniversary. It was the first time in twenty-two years his parents and their three sons had been together as a family—one brother still lives there, the other in New Zealand. An integral part of that reunion was the "do you remember when . . ." stories. When David came back and told the boys these stories, their relationships strengthened as well.

As much as they enjoy hearing stories about their parents, children love to hear (certain) stories about themselves. As children mature, however, some of our favourite stories may no longer be considered appropriate for the telling. When your child asks you not to tell a certain episode, you should immediately stop. There are several stories we hope our children will allow us to tell again as they grow older, but until they say so we can not tell them.

Young children love to hear stories about the day they were born, their first word, their first step, as well as other landmark occasions. These stories demonstrate how each child is unique and special and are reminders of that child's importance. They are also reminders of family links. Often adults hear these stories for the first time when they have their own children—Esther was a very hungry baby and every time Gail's parents came over they would tell her the same story of how famished she always was as a baby.

Some of the stories revolve around things that your children have done or said that you know are worth remembering. One such anecdote took place in Holland when Gail's family were visiting relatives. They were on a boat and Esther, who was quite young at the time, was feeding the ducks, called "*aints*" in Dutch. The next day they returned to the boat. Esther was very excited because she wanted to feed the "isn'ts" again!

Once you have taken a memory and shaped the tale, it "belongs" to the teller. The teller recognizes the worthiness of an incident and decides to shape it into a story, responding to the reactions and responses of the listeners. But it is essential, before you take an incident from your family and tell it as a tale, to remember to get permission from the family members involved. And tell it to *them* before you tell it to *others*. Without that permission, the story should not be told. *Obtaining permission* to tell certain stories, therefore, is an essential element in telling family stories. If you, the teller, were a key player in the event then you do have the right to tell the tale—as long as it does not cause friction with the other key players. However, if it is an event that you only heard about, then ethically you should get permission from those involved first.

Gail takes this maxim very seriously. Not only does she get permission to tell her daughters' personal stories, she asks them for permission to use their creative endeavours. For a school project several years ago, Esther interviewed Gail's father about his experiences in World War II. He told her stories that Gail and her brothers, as children, had refused to listen to—eventually he had stopped telling them. He told Esther of his being shot immediately after landing on the beaches of Normandy on D-Day, his fear as he lay on the beach watching the tide as it began to rise toward the water line which was far beyond his head, his hours of waiting on the cliffs hoping no one in the circle would die. He told, too, of his trip to the British hospital by ship, and of his boots being taken by a uniformed officer who stated that he would never walk again so why would he need the boots? At the hospital he overheard an argument between a nurse and a doctor about the care of the two most seriously wounded men. The doctor suggested the nurse needn't worry too much about them as they would not make it through the night. Her retort was that no one died on her ward and she proceeded to prove it—both men survived—she married the one and the other, Gail's father, came home to Canada. Esther took all the stories told to her during that afternoon and turned them into a creative piece of writing that earned her 100%. Gail asked if she could tell her story of her father's war experiences. Esther said yes, but only if Gail paid her for copyright! Needless to say, since she refused to do so, Gail can only tell the story of how Esther's story came to be.

Keep family stories alive, tell your children the stories your grandparents and parents told you. Ensure that your family history is passed down from generation to generation by saving the stories, either in writing or by having a tape recorder or video camera running while they're being told. Merle can not emphasize too strongly the importance of this, as she wishes she had paid more attention to saving her family's stories. She listened to them and remembers many of them, but memory plays strange tricks, and now that she has no one left to put them in context or confirm details, she wishes she had recorded them, or at least the main points, characters and dates.

Family stories can play an important role in blended families. What better way to get to know and understand one another than through stories? Perhaps start off with the story behind the family names, stories of traditions and rituals that are important to you. Starting new family rituals which combine shared beliefs or traditions help make transitions more comfortable. Family stories are nearly always interrupted with questions or corrections; there is a lack of formality in the telling, yet a feeling of cohesiveness that results.

Merle remembers quite vividly, but without guilt, how much she resented her stepfather's intrusion into her life. Her secure life with her mother's undivided attention was suddenly changed and she was no longer Merle's alone. She also remembers how he removed that resentment. He used to tell her how lazy he was and he thought the best way to become a parent was to find the perfect child. How, being a friend of her father's, he had got to know her, and after her dad had died decided this was the perfect solution. He wanted a child and Merle needed a daddy.

Merle was fortunate as over the years he told her stories about her father, stories of which her mother and grandmother weren't a part. If her stepfather hadn't told them to her, her father would forever have been some mythical person. Instead he was very real and alive to her, and the stories helped her better understand herself. So often the stories came when Merle had either excelled or been very stupid, and her dad would begin, "Did I ever tell you about the time Archie . . .?" She will always be grateful for her stepfather's ability to realize not only how important it was for her to know these stories, but the right time to tell them.

Children often find it far easier to conquer their fears through story. Although successful family integration takes time, and Merle only had to cope with one new parent, sharing stories helped avoid confrontation by breaking down barriers and providing bridges.

For many adults, the highlight of their childhood was hearing stories from their parents or grandparents—there is a bonding which cannot be explained that is generated by stories. A few years ago, Merle was asked to conduct a family storytelling workshop for a one-parent family group. Many of the participants felt they didn't have her ability, but she reassured them by explaining that when she began telling stories to her children, she was no further ahead as a storyteller than they were. "Trust yourselves and give it a try," she suggested. "Choose a short story you know and like, and tell it." A month later, she told stories to the parents and their children at an evening gathering. When she arrived, an eight year old girl went up to thank her for teaching her mother about stories, and to tell her that since that workshop her mother had told her and her younger brother at least one story every day. If they weren't going to be together at night, she made sure she told a story at the breakfast table. The young girl made Merle's day by exclaiming that story-telling was a ritual in their family—and in just one short month!

She often thinks of that family and hopes that storytelling became a ritual when the children were with their father as well. Stories nurture and heal. Children learn that there are really no easy answers, but that problems can be solved if you put your mind to it. They also learn that not every ending is happy, and that by making good choices you have better control.

Unlike Gail's daughters, Merle's sons didn't get to know their grandparents and relatives intimately. Merle and David knew they wanted to keep the communication lines open, and even though Craig was only nine months old when they emigrated, they started taping him learning to talk. Over the years they sent tapes back and forth with the boys telling their stories or asking questions, dinner time conversations, and school concert appearances. In turn their parents sent back tapes with stories for the boys, questions they had about their lives and the different things the boys did. Now, when it is too late, Merle wishes she had had the foresight to keep the tapes and had asked their parents to do the same. Unfortunately, many of their family stories are lost in the mists of time.

If you are fortunate to have access to members of an older generation, do not hesitate to ask questions which can elicit stories.

Often, once this generation is gone, an entire era of historical and family stories is gone as well. Tape the stories and comments if you can. Today many people capture the images and stories on videotape. The way in which you collect and store these stories is not important. What is important is making sure your family stories are preserved.

At times, when we are young, we have no interest at all in the stories of our parents and grandparents. Unfortunately, sometimes it is too late to hear the tales by the time we want and need them.

Not too long ago, Ann Landers' advice column carried a letter from a reader telling how their grandmother had dictated her memories and thoughts into a tape recorder and then asked her daughter to type it up. Now each of her children, grandchildren and generations still to come, have a priceless gift in which she recounted all the milestones of her long life as well as her family genealogy. Sit down by yourself, or with members of your family and tell the stories of "Remember when. . . ." One memory will be the catalyst for the next and soon a treasure chest of memory fragments, stories and emotional ties will be available for all.

Don't forget that to get at the contents of a treasure chest, one needs a key. The key to the treasure chest of priceless family stories is making sure that the tales—the family's history—are recorded for the coming generations to discover.

Section Three

Developing and Learning
To Tell Stories

Stories offer glimpses of the dark and the light for the listener to take away and develop.

Marina Warner

When one listens to a story, one is being creative. The listener adds to it with his or her own imagination.

Arthur T. Allen

Six

SHAPING YOUR STORY

Our objective in this chapter is to explore how easy it is to shape and tell stories in the family. As there are numerous books written for teachers and librarians about learning stories, we are not interested in duplicating that information. Our focus is the process of enlarging a memory, shaping it into a tale and telling it.

It is important to realize that natural storytellers are made, not born. These "natural" tellers take an incident and shape it, smooth it, and deliver it in an unaffected manner which has been perfected through hours and years of practice. The more stories a person tells, the easier it is to develop and tell a new one. Impressive stories are built on understanding and practice. Good storytellers understand, through instinct and groundwork, what makes a good story, how to shape the story so that it is a satisfying listening experience, and how to tell the story effectively.

It is helpful to keep in mind that the easiest stories to tell are the age old tales, folktales like *Cinderella*, *Little Red Riding Hood*, and *The Three Bears*, which have been polished and shaped by generations of tellers and listeners. The basic outlines of these stories have been stretched, embellished and refined by countless voices. Only the best of the old tales are repeated through time and space and, therefore, provide a canon of "good" stories. An added advantage is that these tales belong to the public domain and do not involve any conflict with copyright issues.

Telling simple folktales is good experience for the beginning storyteller. The reasons for this are straightforward: the stories are already in an easy-to-learn format—handed down by generations of storytellers; there are numerous versions of each tale available to modern tellers; and they are fun to tell. Because many of these stories are familiar to the beginning teller, they are good stories with which to start developing storytelling skills. As the content of the tale is already known, the teller only needs to concentrate on the actual narrating of the story.

Remember, no matter what the story, storytelling is TELLING, not memorizing and reciting. But, be sure you save the picture books and literary stories to read to your children as they need a combination of storytelling and reading out loud—both are equally important.

Storytelling comes from deep inside and can only be learned, initially, by trial and error. Merle didn't realize for some time that what she was doing was an artform and had a long history. She explains:

> *I had grown up with unadulterated stories from the African perspective, as well as oral and literary stories from my own British-based culture. After moving to Canada, far from home in a culture that was "somewhat" different from the one I had grown up in, and with two small boys, I intuitively fell back on telling favourite fairy tales from my childhood. I can vaguely remember my first attempts. They weren't great, but as I re-told the stories I discovered the ones that resonated for me. I learned how to play with the story, to tell it my way. Watching my sons' reactions, I discovered what worked and what didn't; I experimented, left out what wasn't working and concentrated on what really meant something to us.*

Years later, when she took her first storytelling course, Merle discovered that her intuition hadn't been too far wrong. Start off with stories you love. If your memory isn't as sharp as you'd like it to be, borrow a collection of folktales from the library and you'll be surprised how quickly the stories come back to you. Choose a really simple tale and tell it. *Goldilocks and the Three Bears* is a good one to start with—it is easy to walk through the story in your mind, and it has a catchy refrain running throughout. Tell it as it is a few times and then start playing with it. Think about the different comparisons you can come up with for "Too hot, Too cold, Too hard, Too soft." The strength of the oral tradition is in the power of appreciating the words, delighting in their use and using them the same way you use crayons or paints. Your choice of words allows both you (the teller) and your listeners to "paint pictures in the mind."

The joy of telling stories to your children is that you challenge yourself and them simultaneously. Play with stories, mix up characters and events, deliberately make mistakes. Children love being able to say "No, that's not the way it goes!" The importance of telling stories you enjoy cannot be overemphasized, especially in the early years, as children love repetition and want to hear the same story over and over again. Merle remembers changing the colours of the hats in *Hats for Sale* to the colours of the rainbow because her sons, Craig and Scott, would argue over the order of the colours each time she told it. To tell the truth, she loved *her* vision of this elongated straight rainbow more! In this old tale, a peddler carries the hats he wishes to sell on top of his head as he travels from town to town. As an organized salesman, he has them arranged by colour— the red ones first and then the blue—or is it the brown and then the yellow? The story is known in picture book format as *Caps for Sale* by Esphyr Slobodkina.

By looking to these traditional folktales, you can learn how your own stories, based on memories and family experiences, can be shaped. Folktales are simple, linear stories involving only a few main characters, with an interesting beginning and plenty of action that quickly builds to a climax. Almost immediately after the climax, the story ends, satisfying the listener. There is not an overabundance of detail or description; the power of the story is in the listener's participation in creating vivid images from the few clues in the tale.

Just as in a folktale, successful personal experience stories do not need unnecessary details, explanations and flashbacks. The secret to a successful story is the fact that it has a point, a reason for the story to be told, something that happens! The event does not have to be earth shattering to be appreciated. So the first questions to ask yourself, when looking at a memory you wish to develop into a story, are:

> *Why should I tell this?*
>
> *What is important about it that others need to know?*
>
> *Will it give the listener an insight into me (the teller), or the main character, or the family itself?*

We are all repositories of memories but sometimes we need a little direction or encouragement to bring some of our memories to the surface. Gail started a file of memory fragments that she thinks of while doing other things. This file is a bank of possible future stories which allows her access into the things she knows she'll always remember and—"what was it again?" Ask yourself some questions to get the memories and thoughts flowing: What was the happiest time you remember or the best gift you ever gave or received and why?

Try to recall the funniest episode that occurred at a family gathering or the scariest or silliest event that ever happened to you. Topics can include reminiscences about your first job, favourite childhood toys, chores that you had to do when you were a child, as well as your favourite pets, sports activities or hobbies. Did you, like Gail's mother, have to walk to school every day regardless of the weather? It was ten miles and up hill both ways! Or have a story like the one about her great-aunt's dog who, when telephones were a rarity, would screen the neighbours who came in to use the phone? If you brought a parcel in with you, you had better show it to the dog before you put it down to use the phone. If you didn't, the dog would not allow you to pick it up again. Think about the stories you heard about characters in the family. What about your first car?

Some memories, however, are as clear as the day they happened. The Christmas Merle was five could have taken place this past year because the memory is still so vivid.

My step-father had been in our family for about sixteen months and, because there were no fir trees in Rhodesia, he made me a Christmas tree, a perfectly symmetrical, picture-book-perfect tree of fresh acacia branches tied over wire netting and wire rings. We could only hang paper chains and a bare minimum of decorations on it as it had to be sprayed daily to keep it alive. On Christmas morning, I noticed that one of my gifts was wrapped very roughly in brown paper and tied with string, no nice paper or neat corners. I left that present for last and when I opened it found a dark blue leather-covered book with gold letters on the front—I can still remember the rich leather smell as well as the feeling of disappointment. Not being able to read, I took the book to dad who opened it up and read what he had written on the fly leaf: "Dear Merle, This is Dic, I hope he becomes your very best friend. Merry Christmas. Love Dad." He closed the book and read out the gold letters "The Oxford Concise Dictionary." Needless to say I wasn't too enthusiastic and paid little attention to the book for the rest of the day. However, that night after my bath, dad lifted me onto his lap in his large comfortable armchair, opened Dic and told me to close my eyes and choose a word.

So began a ritual that was to last many years, of my choosing three words at random each night while dad taught me the intricacies of "reading" a dictionary. He explained the etymology, pronunciation and use of each word. Together we would make up sentences and paragraphs with the new words, pore over the atlas to find the country of origin and, when necessary, dad would read me the myth that gave us that particular word. To this day, dad's "Dic" is the best gift I've ever received because with it he instilled in me a love of words and language.

Not all memories retain this clarity; some must be coaxed from dusty corners in our brain. Hints of possible stories may arrive out of the blue, often while driving on the highway or sitting in the bath. Gail carries a tiny tape recorder with her to make sure these fragments do not slip away. Wet footprints leading from and to the bath are frequently discovered as she finds a pen and paper before she loses that thought! These fragments are added to her file and when she is looking for a story idea she searches through the file to see if any of them are ready to come out and face the light. If so, she begins the process of taking a memory or a fragment of a memory and shaping it into a tellable tale.

To help you in the shaping of your story, Gail has recorded, in the following discussion, the step-by-step process she used in shaping a fragment of a childhood memory into a tellable tale. The following paragraph describes a visual snapshot of this memory fragment.

> *The two passenger trains rested on their respective tracks at the station. One faced east and the other west. Looking out of the window of one of the trains were two children. The oldest, a girl, was about six, her brother, about four. They were waiting for their parents to come back aboard the train. The boy was upset: his sister had told him their parents may not get their coffee in time and that the train would go on without them.*

I would suggest you first take the time to bring back as much of the memory as you can. Recreate it through the use of all five of your senses. Most people depend on their sense of the visual when describing events and characters, but to make a story come alive the teller needs to "duplicate" the experience as much as possible. Use your visual memory but remember to gather the images from your other senses as well.

Often the strongest stimulus for evoking memories and stories is our sense of smell—a new book, spring rain, freshly baked bread! What aromas waft their way through this scene? Cigarette smoke. Coffee. Diesel fumes. The slightly tart smell of Wrigley's gum being chewed by the two children. There is perfume in the air, the hint of fresh laundry, and the smell of leather luggage from the overhead racks.

Closely related to the sense of smell is the sense of taste which is one of the most important senses when constructing family memories. So many family stories begin in the kitchen or at the dinner table. The taste of grandmother's cookies long after she has gone can bring back the times you watched her roll the dough and sprinkle cinnamon in large billowy clouds. On the train in our scene, we have the tang of food and drink being consumed and the taste of the diesel in the air. There is also the taste of dust from the farmers' fields and the taste of excitement, and then fear, in the mouths of the two children.

What sounds could be heard? Conversations from other people in the train car, the people on the platforms and the slightly superior tone of the know-it-all sister as she prepares to terrify, once again, her poor brother. It is October, a fine clear day on the Canadian prairies, and the geese overhead are honking their farewells. There is clanking of dishes and crackling of chocolate bar wrappers in the train car, and the conductor and brakeman are chattering outside the next window. The east-bound train actually leaves about this time and so train car and engine noises hang over the other sounds.

The sense of touch brings the warmth of the sun shining through the window, the sticky seats kept warm by two wriggling bodies, and the children clinging to each other as they stare horrified out the far window as the train gathers speed and leaves the station.

To develop these images into a full story, I go through the exercise of gathering all the images I can, not necessarily because I want to include them in my story, but in order to more completely visualize the action and the characters involved. While the characters do not need to be fully developed in order for this story to be effective, it is essential the listener knows the children are young and the older sibling feels superior to her younger brother. Because I knew these characters very well (my brother and myself), I did not have to go through an imaging exercise, but when I wish to tell a story about someone I don't know well, I spend time discovering the characters and getting to know them. I am not looking at physical characteristics so much as emotional traits. I take each character out of the story (memory) and "stand them on a pedestal," then walk around them, studying the way they stand and move. Are they graceful? Awkward? Stoop-shouldered from years of hard, back-breaking labour? Because eyes, mouths and hands are the first things I focus on when meeting "real" people, I concentrate on the same features with each of my characters. Do their lips curve naturally into a smile? Are laugh-lines in evidence around the eyes? Do their fingers have callouses or are they smooth and soft? How do they sound when they speak? Gruff? Educated? Timid?

While none of these details may be central to the story, they are essential to the success of the telling. Unless the storyteller can clearly see the characters move, speak and act, it is extremely difficult to bring them alive to a listening audience.

One of the first exercises my storytelling students undertake is the analysis of characters from stories. I am concerned about three aspects: character traits, motivation of the character, and purpose of the character in the story. The physical attributes are important only when they are necessary for the story—Rapunzel needs her long braids for the story to work!

Character traits allow insights into the type of person the character is and therefore how she or he may react in certain situations. Is the character honest? Stingy? Confident? Overbearing? Frequently character traits can be deciphered from the content of the story, but just as often it is left to the teller to develop a satisfactory character. Because you, as storyteller, have "unveiled" these people and understand how they will act in a given situation (based on their character traits), the audience can also "see" them and accept their behaviour as natural to the character.

Let us return to the snapshot and pull the two children out and set them on their pedestals.

> *The little girl is extremely bossy with an air of self-confidence and self-importance—after all she is in charge of her little brother (and of the situation?). She is also mischievous. Her brother trusts his older sister, but with reservations. Both are bundles of energy and excitement.*

Next we turn to the motivation of the characters—what makes them tick? Why are they reacting in that manner while other characters are not? What else would they do? If the character is essentially greedy, he or she may react to the reading of a will quite differently from someone living in a cloister! Cinderella's two step-sisters are jealous of Cinderella's beauty and, because they are spoiled and self-centred, react to her with malice. If they were motivated by anything else, we would have a different story!

> *The little girl is bored by the enforced inactivity. She loves to be centre of attention as well as to tease her brother. Her brother, on the other hand, dislikes any attention. He depends on his sister to take care of him in public situations.*

Why is the character in the story? What purpose does he or she play? Major character or minor character? Catalyst for the action? Necessary for the action to take place? Observer?

> *Both children are major characters in this story. The little boy also acts as a catalyst for the action— without his reaction to his sister's comments there would be no story.*

Additional characters we will meet during the rest of the story are a mother, a father, and an "invisible" train porter. For each of these characters, I go through this same exploration: Who are these people? What motivates them? What is their purpose in *this* story?

Another important consideration is point-of-view. Who is telling the story? Is it one of the characters or an impartial observer? Is the character telling it as it happens, or as an older person looking back at the past? Point-of-view can change the story substantially. When teaching storytelling, I divide my class into large groups and give each group a different character from the same story. Each group discovers their character's traits, motivation, and purpose in the story and then tells the story to the rest of the class from that character's point-of-view. Depending on the number of characters (and groups), we hear a variety of *different* stories! The wolf, who was framed and arrested because he attacked the third little pig who had insulted his grandmother in *The True Story of the Three Little Pigs*, tells a much different tale than most of us have heard before.

How much detail do you need to include in order for the listener to know the person in the tale? If it is a family member with whom the audience is familiar, then very little needs to be said about the character. But what if it is someone who is distant to them through time and/or space? Because the aim of the story is to effectively communicate the point that the teller wishes to make, the story needs to become relevant to the listeners. The story must contain just enough detail to help the audience understand the situation being brought to life. The actual details included in the telling are dependent upon the content of the story and the particular audience. For example, a story about Uncle John who has always lived down the road from your house won't need a great amount of detail to bring Uncle John alive in a story told about him to your children. But what if you were telling the same incident to someone who had never met Uncle John? What other details would be needed for that audience to understand the tale? Is it important for them to know that Uncle John is only five feet tall? Or that he eats soup with a fork? While these details may fascinate you, unless they are pertinent to the story they do not need to be included —until you are telling a story about Uncle John's experiences at the dinner table.

I suggest first writing down as many of the impressions as you can remember regardless of their importance to the actual story. The next step is to decide which of these points or impressions are really necessary to make the story you want to tell satisfying and effective. Any that do not enhance the audiences' understanding of the characters, the setting, or the series of events within the tale should be discarded. This is what makes folktales so effective and memorable—only the necessary details are handed down and retold. While some details fascinate you or make you laugh, they may not be appropriate for this story. In fact, they may distract the listener entirely. We have all experienced someone interrupting their story with an audible but internal dialogue about, for example, whether the spring that year was wet or dry, when the information has nothing to do with the particular story.

It may be important to pay attention to the setting of the story. Certain tales are timeless and placeless—they can take place anytime and anywhere. Other tales need to have the time and place firmly established in the minds of the listeners in order for them to fully understand what they are hearing. This is particularly important in stories about women and their actions, for example. If the story takes place in the past and you do not make this clear to the audience, some may resent what you are saying and decide you are demonstrating antiquated values and attitudes. We should never revise history but, in order to learn from it, listeners need to know that what they are hearing encompasses historical values and attitudes regardless of modern feelings about the subject. In the "snapshot" we have been discussing, it is important to establish that the parents were not negligent leaving the children behind in the train car—the porter was informed of their departure and parents in those times did not have the same worries about their children as they do today. In fact, now that I am a parent I can fully appreciate their desire for a few minutes peace and quiet!

Once the memory is fresh and clear in your mind, ask yourself a very important question: how does this begin? In order to have a developed story, rather than a meandering group of impressions, you need to shape the memory into a story structure. Once you decide how the story begins, you can fashion the rest of the tale.

The introduction to a story is an integral part of its success. Stories should always begin with a powerful and intriguing beginning, something that hooks the listener into wanting to know more, to hear more, now! As in any story, the beginning of a family tale must introduce the characters, the setting (both time and place), and the problem. Without a problem, crisis or humourous situation, there is no story. Also, make sure the ending is strong, satisfying the listener with the way problems were solved and questions were answered. This does not mean that all stories need to end " . . . and they lived happily ever after." But the ending does need to address all of the conflicts introduced in the beginning of the story.

The series of events leading from the introduction, through the climax, to the conclusion needs to be fairly linear—with action, and consequences following the action. This is not the place for flashbacks, elaborate descriptions, or digressions.

If you write your story out, do not bother about full sentences but rather work on a broad outline of events. Working with full text fosters an anxiety that you may forget a word—so you memorize the words rather than concentrate on telling what actually happened in the story. Working with an outline allows the teller to focus on making the action come alive, instead of on individual words. The following outline would be all I would normally record on paper before learning the present tale.

Introduction: Characters: me, Ivan, mom, dad
                  Setting: train, early 1950s, Canadian
                            prairie town
                  Problem: alone on train, waiting for mom and
                            dad, second train leaves station

Initial action: decision to trick Ivan
Next events: bring train to Ivan's attention, watch as he
              becomes agitated and then truly frightened
Climax: contagious reaction, mom and dad return,
         coffee stain
Conclusion: all is well, I knew it all the time!

Because this book is a written "performance," a full text sequence of the story follows to demonstrate how the outline may be "fleshed out" or embellished and brought to life.

I always loved to tease my little brother. It was something I excelled at; something I always took great pride in doing well. So what if I got into trouble with my parents—it was worth every minute of it!

Sometimes, however, my teasing ran away with me—just like the train. . . .

The train stop was in the middle of Saskatchewan somewhere and people were moving around in the train and outside on the platform. Mom and dad told Ivan and me to stay put, they were going off the train for a few minutes and would bring us back a treat. A treat! We bounced up and down on the seat trying to guess what they would bring us . . . I was hoping for a toy but Ivan was sure it was going to be something to eat. Suddenly the constant clatter around us was shattered by the noises of a train about to leave the station. The whistle blew! The conductor shouted: "All Aboard!" and the wheels started to screech against the rails. Children plastered their foreheads to the windows and the last few stragglers came running down the platform. There were shouts of laughter and excitement right outside our window. Right! I knew that it was the train on the next set of tracks, but you know, it sure looked like it was our train that was moving! Ivan was only four, he didn't know much at all . . . so . . .

"Look, Ivan, the train is going without mommy and daddy!"

He stared out the window as the train started to move faster. He looked at me and then, as the train gathered speed, he started to scream. There was so much noise already, but his scream was louder than anything I have ever heard. He sobbed and screamed and . . . I started to get scared! I looked out the window. Maybe it was our train that was moving. Oh no! It was! "Mommy!" "Daddy!" I joined Ivan in his hysteria.

Mom and dad heard us from the coffee bar and started to run towards our stationary train. The coffee spilled before they reached the steps. As mom stood over us in complete dismay, I saw the coffee stain all

down her new dress. I cried even louder! Finally,
they grabbed us and held us close until we stopped
bellowing and calmed down.

> *"I knew it wasn't our train!" I kept insisting later.*
> *"I just said it to scare Ivan. I knew you wouldn't leave*
> *us." But, you know, just for a few minutes, I wasn't*
> *completely sure!*

This event is vivid in my memory, not only because it was quite traumatic but also because it has been reinforced numerous times over the years as my parents have told it again and again. At each retelling, images and rationale have been expanded. We were not abandoned; the porter had been asked to keep an eye on us but stood by helplessly as our horror spiralled. One of my strongest images is of my mother, in a rush to get to us, spilling her coffee all down the front of her dress. I learned much later it was a new dress, worn for the first time, and the coffee stain would not come out. Mom never wore the dress again. My parents used this story to illustrate my sisterly qualities every time my two daughters fought and teased each other. It was also told as a transition tale, part of the story of our move from Manitoba to Alberta.

I do not incorporate all the details and images that I consciously sought, but when I tell the story to others, I feel that I am back in that train, a child of six, and in the middle of an adventure.

Remember that stories are not created as perfected tales without preliminary work and that some of this work includes practicing telling the tale to someone to watch their response and hear their evaluation. What worked in the story and why? What did not and why? Take the recommendations and refine your story. Tell it again to the same audience and perhaps to someone new. How does it work now? Stories told without careful thought are often filled with unnecessary details that bog down the teller ("Was it in the fall of 1959 or 1960? No, I think it was the spring of 1961.") and the listener ("This has nothing to do with the story. I have better things to do than to listen to this rambling!") Stories told without a point are meaningless. And stories told without skill are often lost on audiences who are "trained" not to listen when people are talking.

Sometimes you can forget to put important points into the tale in your enthusiasm to tell the story. My father became excited one day while I was telling stories at Fort Edmonton Historical Park. The Park had just acquired a reconditioned truck identical to the first truck his father bought. Dad told me the story of the day he first saw his father's truck and I asked his permission to tell the story to others. This he readily gave and I told the tale to my next audience. When I finished, they looked at me rather strangely because I had forgotten an important part of the story. As a result it did not make a lot of sense to them. I use this experience in workshops to show that *some* details really are important.

> *My grandfather came to Canada from Russia as a*
> *young man with one desire, to own land. Because as*
> *a Jew he had not been allowed to own the land, he*
> *knew very little about it before coming here. Because*
> *of this, the land he eventually owned produced one*
> *very large bumper crop each year—rocks—and not*
> *much else. Soon, instead of planting grain, he began*
> *to raise chickens and horses. He enjoyed working*
> *with horses: he broke them for the neighbours, rode*
> *them, raced them and used them to pull his wagon*
> *as he sold his eggs. One day he decided it was time*
> *to become a modern farmer, a progressive farmer.*
> *He was going to buy a truck. He took his savings and*
> *went into town where he purchased a truck and,*
> *because he was very short and could not see over*
> *the steering wheel, a pillow. He started on the*
> *journey home. My grandmother, father, and all his*

*brothers were standing on the front porch anxiously
awaiting his arrival. They saw the truck coming down
the road, saw my grandfather's proud grin and
gleaming eyes. They watched as he turned into the
farm yard and headed towards them. My grandfather's grin grew even wider and his eyes sparkled
with pride and excitement. Just before he reached
the porch he held very tightly to the steering wheel
and yelled, "Whoa, back!" But the truck kept on going
and struck the corner of the porch before it stalled
and stopped. My grandmother, father and uncles
managed to get out of harm's way and, when my
grandfather eventually pulled himself up from the
floor well of the truck where he had landed after
slipping off the pillow, he was very sheepish. After
making sure no one was hurt, he fixed the porch.
The truck always had a big dent in it.*

When I first told this tale to the people at Fort Edmonton,
I forgot to mention anything about horses—they had no
idea why he wouldn't step on the brake instead of pulling
back on the reins. When I tell the story now, there are
many details that were not in my father's telling, but have
become part of the tale because, to me, it is important they
should be there! The pillow is totally my addition because
I love the image of my grandfather sliding off the pillow
into the floor well while his grin slides off his face. It is a
scene I see in full Technicolor, but it happens only in my
imagination. When I tell this story I meet many people
whose parents and grandparents had the same experience
as they switched from horses to cars. A truly western
family tale!

I don't put many details about *my* grandfather into the
tale because the power of a story is the image created in
the mind of the listener—usually the likeness of their own
grandfather. The part about his being short does not have
to be included for the story to work, but as neither my

father nor I are very tall, it is one way to identify with our family heritage.

Several points should be made here. To tell a really effective story, some preparation is necessary, but most family tales are told spontaneously, without prior preparation time. "That reminds me of my grandfather. . . ." It is important to tell stories when the time is right. They should not be ignored because you have had no time to reflect on the memory and all that it entails. What happens, however, is that after you have had some experience working with your memories over time, and developing them into tellable tales, other memories will be unconsciously structured as they are told, making a "found" instance into a "developing" story that can be polished as you tell it again.

The appropriate length of the story is one concern often voiced at our workshops. The tales we tell range from one minute to twenty to thirty minutes in length. Stories do not have to be long and complicated to be effective, but they must be carefully moulded into a tellable tale, and then told with some skill to be truly effective.

While the process of shaping a story can be time consuming, it is truly a pleasurable experience. There are numerous side benefits to taking a memory and breathing life into it: you learn more about members of your family, yourself, and your environment. You may delve into the memories of other family members while exploring your own memories; do not be surprised when these memories do not always correspond to your own. But the greatest pleasure of all is the creation of a legacy, in story form, that lives on and on.

From mouth to ear to mouth the old tales went.

Jane Yolen

SEVEN

TELLING YOUR STORY

T he art of telling a story involves much more than saying a series of words. While the words are important, the story-teller's use of natural body movements, facial and hand gestures and the voice are of vital consideration. Don't be alarmed. We do not mean you have to dramatize the story as if you are appearing on stage. Watch people around you while they are having a conversation. Their faces glow or glower, depending on the tone of the dialogue; their arms and hands move, gesturing to the listener in an attempt to give more force to the words and images they are trying to convey; and their eyes focus on the eyes of their listeners. They lean into the conversation (as do their attentive listeners) and their voices range through several pitches as well as travel at different speeds. When they get to the exciting part—in the climax—their speech gets faster, often louder, as they communicate the point of the anecdote. Listen to the way pauses are used to add drama, suspense, or humour before delivering the punchline of a joke or story. There is no pressure from the audience to provide a polished performance—the listeners are enjoying the pictures created by the teller. This is exactly what should happen when you are telling a "prepared" story. The most effective storyteller is the one who looks and sounds as if storytelling is an effortless activity.

When the storyteller thoroughly enjoys the story and can see the characters, setting and action clearly in his or her own mind while telling the story, much of the art of storytelling comes naturally.

Most people automatically make use of their hands, body and face to help them communicate an idea or story or to replace dialogue. "Yes" and "no" are frequently communicated by the appropriate shake of the head. A person scolding a child often shakes their finger—"no." "Come here," "I don't know," "stop," and "over there" are only a few examples of statements that can be communicated without words. These gestures can be easily and effectively employed when telling your tales—the danger may be in using them too emphatically or too often. In today's world of visual stimulation, audiences may watch your hands instead of focusing on what you are saying. We recommend loose clothing with large comfortable pockets to hide your hands if you are prone to waving them around energetically. Another word of warning. Gestures should be well timed, slightly anticipating your words rather than following them. Otherwise, the story and action are slightly out of kilter, leaving the listener dissatisfied without knowing why. In order to be as effective as possible, we practice and practice our gestures until they become "spontaneous."

Several aspects of voice are important considerations when telling stories. *Rate*, the number of words spoken per minute, varies according to the age of the character speaking, the type of action taking place, and the nervousness of the storyteller. Effective storytelling involves fluctuating rate. Older people usually speak with a slower rate while young children have a much faster rate of speech. Utilize this fact when your characters are speaking; dialogue will sound natural and authentic. Most beginning storytellers speak at a rate that is much too fast; they sound as if they can't wait to get to the end of the story. Slow down between ideas—not words.

Make use of the *pause* to vary your rate of speech and to heighten suspense when telling your tales. "What is going to happen next? Shhh! Be quiet, I want to hear." A common fault with beginning storytellers or nervous presenters is filling the pauses with "and so," "and ah," and so on. The listeners need the silences between the ideas and settings they are hearing in order to understand what they are being told. The effective use of the pause is possibly the most powerful tool a teller has. A good demonstration of this is borrowed from a workshop by storyteller Ruth Stotter. To hear how pauses can alter meaning say the following sentence aloud. *The little girl went into the forest.* Repeat the sentence with a pause between "the" and "little." Between "little" and "girl." Listen to the different meanings of this one sentence as you complete this exercise, putting pauses between the other words in the sentence.

Pitch refers to the "highness" or "lowness" of the voice. Variations in pitch help bring the story and the characters alive. Practice changes of pitch when you are telling the story of *The Three Bears.* "Some one has been eating my porridge," (said Papa Bear in a deep gruff pitch). "Some one has been eating my porridge," (said Mama Bear in a low mellow pitch). "Some one has been eating my porridge," (said Baby Bear in a high squeaky pitch), "and they ate it all up!" By changing your pitch, and keeping it consistent for the different characters throughout the story, the teller does not have to identify the character by saying "Baby Bear said" each time that character has a speaking part. The listener automatically understands who is speaking.

Another important consideration is uniform *volume.* It may seem obvious that the story must be told in a voice that all the listeners can easily hear, but many of us have developed the unfortunate habit of "swallowing" the ends of sentences. Be sure all the words can be heard. Also remember a whisper can be more powerful than a shout when trying to get someone's attention. But the whisper must be audible as well. When we are nervous we tend to speak quietly, and often to our shoes or the ceiling—but our listeners are not there. Direct your voice to the ears of your audience and make sure all can hear you adequately.

Vocal energy is vital if you are telling stories to young children. This does not mean you have to be loud and boisterous, but rather, it means infusing your words with life and vitality. Regardless of the reason you are telling them a story, you want them to attend to you at that moment. Vocal energy ensures that their interest will be caught and maintained. It is also important for adult audiences as well. Everyone likes a good story—well told.

A beginner's biggest fear is that they'll forget something important as they tell the story. Don't worry about it! The important thing is to keep the story moving, and since you are telling, not reciting the story, you can make a slight detour and say "did I mention . . ." or "what she had forgotten until this instance was. . . ." If you leave something important out of a story your children know well, they will tell you. You can then praise them for being such good listeners and never have to acknowledge you hadn't intended to tell the story that way. Just remember, it's your story, and sometimes the little imperfections are what give it the personal touch.

Selection of an appropriate story for the age and interest level of your intended audience is the best insurance for success. While young children may listen attentively, for a short period of time, to a story that is intended for an older audience, adolescents rarely are so polite. We often tell stories to mixed age groups and have learned to inform each age level that we will tell a story especially for them later. The following guidelines may be useful.

There are elements in the stories and the telling that appeal to the youngest listeners. Like the rhythm in nursery rhymes, the stories should flow and dance with the child's internal beat. Include refrains that are fun to say and repeat with the child. Young children love sound effects such as the *ding dong* of the doorbell and the *mooing* of the cow. One old tale that is extremely satisfying with young listeners is the story of "*The Bear* (or Lion) *Hunt*" with the *swishy swishy* of walking through the grass, the *squelch* of walking through the mud and so on (Rosen, *Going on a Bear Hunt*). Young children also appreciate nonsense. They love silliness in stories, hearing about people putting animals in their bed to help them sleep (Lottridge, *Ten Small Tales*), or the Fat Cat eating all and everyone in sight (Kent, *Fat Cat*). They are also fond of stories about characters reacting "literally" to the familiar sayings in the English language. They enjoy nonsense words and the chance to laugh with their favourite people. They are not critical listeners and are not concerned with your technique. They are just happy to be sharing a pleasurable moment of your busy day.

As children grow older, they still enjoy your tales although they become a more demanding audience and request tales with action and drama. Often, as they reach their teenage years, they seem to not want to hear your stories. As a teenager, Gail confesses, she decided not to listen to her dad's war experiences anymore but when he told her other stories she was riveted to his words. The secret, therefore, is to find appropriate stories for each interest level. The teenage years are the time for personal experience tales, the stories of you at that age, stories which reflect their anxiety about the world and their place in it, the stories and emotions that fuse a bond across the generations.

As your children reach adulthood and become parents themselves, the selection of stories changes again. They still want to hear personal experience stories but they often want to reach further into the past, discovering or rediscovering their family heritage. Gail is extremely grateful her daughters have had the chance to be active members of an extended family. They know both sets of grandparents very well and have sat at all four sets of knees to hear stories. Not all children are so fortunate. Gail, herself, grew up within easy reach of one set of grandparents and had family reunions every second year with her uncles, aunts and cousins. Peter did not know his *Oma* (grandmother) until he was a teenager when she arrived in Canada for her first visit. He and his Oma did not speak a common language, but through the stories told by his parents Peter knows his relatives—both those who are living and those several generations in the past.

The time we take to tell stories to our children is one of the most profitable investments that we can make. Do not hesitate. Jump in and tell a story today. Regardless of the length of the tale or your concept of your performing abilities, tell them something that will make them laugh, see you in a different light, and connect the generations. There is no one right age for a child to begin to listen to your stories—the right age is the age your child is now.

In our attempt to unlock the storyteller in every one of you, we can only offer encouragement. You will never be comfortable telling stories if you worry about it. As you have probably told your own children, practice makes it easier, "Rome was not built in a day," "Wayne Gretzky had to learn to skate first," "practice makes—it possible."

SECTION FOUR
UNIVERSAL TALES

When an old person dies, a whole library disappears.

African proverb

I'll tell you a story
About Jack a Nory,
And now my story's begun;
I'll tell you another
Of Jack and his brother,
And now my story is done.

EIGHT

NURSERY RHYMES

Nursery rhymes are nuggets of gold—oral treasures that have been passed on from generation to generation. Each rhyme is a tiny story, complete with beginning, middle, and end, and a perfect rhythm which was originally recited by, and for, adults for centuries. Many can be traced back to stories and anecdotes about historical people and events. However, their strength today lies in the fact that over the years, through constant re-telling, they have been polished and smoothed into perfectly paced miniature stories. They are a wonderful introduction to language and the way words come alive when spoken.

That nursery rhymes were not originally meant only for the very young is born out by Iona and Peter Opie, co-authors of *The Oxford Dictionary of Nursery Rhymes*. They conducted intensive research into the origins of the rhymes and came to the conclusion that the rhymes started off as adult fare—political satire, snippets of ballads and old customs.

Mary, Queen of Scots, for example, was apparently a fashion plate who ordered beautiful gowns from France—some of which were decorated with gold-plated sea-shells while others had tiny silver bells attached to the hems. Knowing this, it is easy to believe that this rhyme:

> *Mary, Mary, quite contrary*
> *How does your garden grow?*
> *With silver bells and cockle shells*
> *And pretty maids all in a row.*

was referring to this controversial queen.

The Bishop of Glastonbury, responsible for the title deeds of the estates in Glastonbury, sent twelve title deeds to King Henry VIII with his steward Jack Horner. For safety, they were carried in an empty Christmas pie shell. However, only eleven arrived at journey's end. Jack Horner "pulled" one and kept it! The Horner family still own the estate at Mells Park in England. It's easy to imagine with what feeling a court jester would recite:

> *Little Jack Horner*
> *Sat in a corner*
> *Eating his Christmas pie.*
> *He put in his thumb*
> *And pulled out a plum*
> *And said "What a good boy am I!"*

Dr. John Fell, who was Dean of Christchurch at Oxford in the late 1600s was known as a strict disciplinarian. One student who faced expulsion from Dr. Fell was told he could remain if he could extemporaneously translate a Latin verse. His spontaneous and daring rendering, which allowed him to stay at Christchurch, is still used as a way of showing utter dislike.

> *I do not like thee Dr. Fell.*
> *The reason why I cannot tell*
> *But this I know, and know full well*
> *I do not like thee Dr. Fell.*

It matters not to children how long ago these rhymes were first recited, or why; what they enjoy is the shared intimacy and sheer delight of the words.

No discussion about nursery rhymes would be complete without mention of Mother Goose. Who was this mythical old woman? Some researchers believe she can be traced back to the 700s, to Charlemagne's mother "Goose-Footed Bertha," so nicknamed because she had skin webs between her toes. She also had an affection for the rhymes recited by court jesters and troubadours poking fun at royalty.

The first known use of Mother Goose in relation to children's stories or nursery rhymes was in Charles Perrault's *Stories and Tales of Past Times with Morals, or Tales of Mother Goose*. This was published in French in 1697 and contained eight stories but no rhymes. It was translated into English by Robert Sambers in 1727. John Newberry, the first British publisher of children's books, brought out a small illustrated book in 1760, *Mother Goose's Melody*, which included fifty-two rhymes from folklore and fifteen songs from Shakespeare's plays.

There is also a possible North American connection, but one that has never been proven. Apparently an Elizabeth Goose lived in Boston, Massachusetts in the early 1700s. She married a widower with ten children and had six of her own. In 1719, one of her sons-in-law published a booklet of her songs and nursery rhymes titled *Songs for the Nursery or Mother Goose's Melodies*. No copies of the book have ever been found, although there are several graves with the last name Goose in the Boston area.

Some songs and rhymes are found internationally. Gail's mother-in-law sang and recited the Dutch songs and rhymes she had heard as a child and used with her own children in Canada. All of the grandchildren know something of the Dutch language as a result of this special time with their *Oma* (grandmother). Gail's parents shared with their granddaughters the Yiddish rhymes with which they were familiar from their childhood. Both girls, when entering French-immersion kindergarten, found learning another language extremely easy and familiar as they had a firm foundation of listening to different sounds.

Every culture has its own collection of nursery rhymes and songs, and it is extremely important that these are also passed on to children. Unfortunately, because the rhyme and rhythm of the words are often lost in translation, few are available in English. During the eleven years the Parent-Child Mother Goose Program has been running in Toronto its leaders have been collecting and adapting rhymes from other cultures through its participants.They will soon be publishing a much-needed book containing the results of this venture. The book will not only have the rhymes in their original languages with an English adaptation, but they will have been smoothed and perfected through the years they have been tested with parents and children.

One of the most important aspects of nursery rhymes is that it is impossible to tell them in anything but a loving or happy voice. No matter how tense or tired you are, when reciting nursery rhymes you automatically relax as the words start rolling off your tongue. The rhythm and cadence of the rhymes injects warmth and security into your voice and this has an effect on both child and teller.

When Merle was pregnant with her first son, the memories of being "Mother Goosed" by all the adults in her family surfaced. Some rhymes came virtually unbidden such as

Ring the bell	pull gently on hair
Knock at the door	knock on forehead
Peep in	look into eyes
Lift the latch	push up tip of nose
Walk in	knock gently on teeth
Let's go down to the cellar	tickle down throat
And eat apples	tickle tummy

She spent a wonderful six months reacquainting herself with remembered rhymes and others long forgotten, leafing through book after book and reciting them out loud to her ever expanding stomach. She wonders how, growing up in the heat of Africa, she had been quite at home with:

> *Snow, snow faster,*
> *Ally-ally blaster;*
> *The Old woman's plucking her geese,*
> *Selling the feathers a penny a piece.*

even though she had no idea whatsoever what snow was. This is, however an image her sons identified with growing up in Canada! One of the benefits of this reacquaintance with nursery rhymes was after her first child, Craig arrived. Whenever he or she, was testy, she didn't need to use books because many rhymes were stored in her brain ready to recite when needed. Her arms and hands were ready to hold, play with or comfort him. The rhyme she used most often during the years her sons were growing up was one her grandmother regularly recited to her:

> *The moon is round,*
> *As round can be,*
> *Two eyes, a nose,*
> *And a mouth like me.*

It was the first rhyme she recited when she first held her newborn sons and traced their beautiful faces ever so gently with her finger. She used it time and time again during their growing-up years—to soothe, to wash wriggly faces, to wipe runny noses they hated having touched, and to introduce a twenty-two month-old to his new brother, with his little hands tracing the now familiar pattern.

Nursery rhymes are like that. They make connections to a time long past and allow you to use language in all its beauty with newborns and toddlers, to talk to them as the little human beings they are. No baby talk, just good language with a rhythm. Because of this strong, evocative language, you ensure, from the beginning, your children are learning to interact through language, and are constructing a solid foundation. It seems so pointless to use diminutives that will no longer be considered acceptable or cute once children reach about age four. Far better to use words which will stimulate their imaginations and which they will be able to use in the future.

"There Was An Old Woman Tossed up in a Basket" was a favourite rhyme of Merle's as a child, long before anyone thought sending someone up in space would be practical. Her sons also loved it and would gaze at the moon to see if the cobwebs had been brushed off. One of the beauties of this rhyme dating back to the mid-1640s, is that three hundred and fifty years later the words have more relevance than when they were first recited.

> There was an old woman tossed up in a basket
> Seventy times as high as the moon;
> And where she was going I couldn't but ask it,
> For in her hand she carried a broom.
>
> Old woman, old woman, old woman, quoth I,
> O whither, O whither, O whither so high?
> To brush the cobwebs off the sky!
> Shall I go with thee? Ay, by and by.

Nursery rhymes are a cost-free entertainment and learning package all bundled into one. They strengthen the bond between parent and child, de-stress the teller and listener, and gently introduce babies to language and memory development.

Language is the essential tool of learning; it is what allows us to think abstractly and make decisions, to store in the brain a comprehension base or a list of criteria on which to draw to reach conclusions. Research shows that nearly fifty percent of one's intelligence is fully developed by the age of four, with another thirty percent by age eight. The remaining twenty percent is built upon this foundation. Oral language is the centre of all communication and storytelling is the original "information superhighway."

Very little children hear and identify with sounds such as the *squish, squish* of squelching through mud; revel in the action of bouncing up and down; and they begin that wonderful understanding of language. Children pick up on refrains very easily and will chime in "I'll do it myself" or "can't catch me . . ." without any urging.

Babies are able to process sound from a very early age and they respond to and identify with many sounds. A tiny baby will turn to a mother's voice in a roomful of other voices. Language, its rhythm and cadence, evokes responses from the beginning—responses to joy and sorrow. Some scholars refer to rhyme as *motherese* because it is the universal language used by mothers (and fathers) in early childhood. Babies identify with the rhythm, not the rhyme, and feel secure because of its gentle sing-song sound.

Before they can begin to learn to read and write, children need a basic vocabulary and understanding of language. Without some experience of how words sound and what they mean, letters on a page will take much longer to understand. Starting with nursery rhymes and lullabies and moving on to simple stories, children learn to create mental images from words, to use their imaginations, to connect patterns and to understand metaphors and similes. In fact, James Reaney, a professor of Canadian Literature at the University of Western Ontario, is convinced all students need a solid foundation of nursery rhymes. He feels if one understands nursery rhymes, one can analyze contemporary literature because the nursery rhymes contain all the devices of literature—symbolism, myth, and so on.

This solid foundation of nursery rhymes involves small children in the two-way process of communication. They absorb the sounds that surround them and, although they don't try, as we adults do, to translate or understand exactly what the words mean, through repetition the language becomes alive and they begin to recognize the words. Later, when they are introduced to the picture books of the rhymes and stories you have recited and told, they will find it easier to scan the text and learn to predict and interpret. Children love to find their favourite rhymes and stories in a picture book and they will discuss how their mental images differ from the actual pictures.

Here are two nursery rhymes in which three-year-olds changed the words to fit their interpretations:

> *Humpty Dumpty sat on a wall.*
> *Humpty Dumpty had a great fall.*
> *All the kings horses and all the king's men*
> *Had scrambled eggs for breakfast again.*

and

> *Pat-a-cake, pat-a-cake*
> *Baker's man,*
> *Bake me a cake*
> *As fast as you can.*
> *Pat it and prick it*
> *And mark it with a B,*
> *Then throw it in the microwave*
> *For baby and me.*

The second one also demonstrates that ancient rhyme and modern technology go hand-in-hand in a child's mind.

Listening to nursery rhymes gets the imagination working. The repetition allows the baby or child to become accustomed to the sounds and the actions, and to take ownership of the rhymes. A friend of ours tells this story of her three-year-old nephew. They were sitting discussing body parts one day and she turned his hand over and explained "This is your palm." "No, it's not!" was his definite reply. "But it is your palm." He was equally adamant it wasn't. "Well, if it isn't your palm, what is it?" "It's my round and round the garden."

Round and round the garden	Trace circles in palm of
Went the teddy bear	child's hand
One step,	Slowly walk fingers up arm
Two steps,	
Tickly under there.	Gently tickle under the arm.

"Round and Round the Garden" is a rhyme parents from around the world, and in many languages, recite and play with their children. Often one doesn't understand the words, just the actions and the universal delighted response from the child.

Many early rhymes were riddles, again asked of adults by adults. "Humpty Dumpty" is a prime example. Before the advent of picture books, listeners had to guess what Humpty was. Something that could not be repaired by either the very strong or the very wise. Without illustrations, deciding it was an egg was not that simple.

Other favourite riddles from years ago which children today still enjoy are:

> *Little Nancy Etticoat,*
> *With a white petticoat,*
> *And a red nose;*
> *She has no feet or hands,*
> *The longer she stands,*
> *The shorter she grows.*　　　　(candle)

and this one which children get straight away but adults oftentimes have problems solving:

> *Four stiff-standers*
> *Four dilly-danders*
> *Two lookers*
> *Two crookers*
> *And a wig wag.*　　　　(cow)

There is an African riddle Merle learned as a child for which there is a British counterpart, and she's sure the riddle is asked in other countries as well.

> *My father's cattle are all white*
> *with a red bull.*　　　　(teeth and tongue, African)

> *Thirty white horses*
> *Upon a red hill*
> *Now they tramp.*
> *Now they champ.*
> *Now they stand still.*　　　　(teeth and gums, British)

Action rhymes are marvellous sanity savers when babies or toddlers are getting frustrated or balking at doing something. Not only do they distract the baby, but the adult as well! There are often times when babies wriggle when you're changing diapers, or toddlers just don't want to get in the bathtub. These normally occur at a time when one's patience is running thin. Rather than getting bad tempered, recite a nursery rhyme and include actions to suit the purpose.

Leg over leg,	cross legs over and over
The dog went to Dover,	
When he came to a stile,	
Whoops! He went over.	lift into tub, or remove diaper

You cross their legs over and over, lift them up and remove or replace a diaper, or over the tub and gently lower them into the water. In both instances you can continue to repeat the rhyme and actions as long as necessary.

This one is great for helping parents keep their cool when a toddler is being overly persistent about something. Take the child on your knees facing you and recite this popular bouncing rhyme complete with actions:

Father and mother and Uncle John	
Went to market, one by one	bounce up and down gently
Father fell off	slide child off to left
And mother fell off	slide child off to right
But Uncle John went on and on	
and on and on. . . .	continue bouncing

When you're in lineups with a fussing baby or toddler you can recite:

This little pig went to market,	pull on toes or fingers from
This little pig stayed at home,	big toe/thumb down
This little pig had roast beef,	
This little pig had none,	

> *And this little pig cried*
> *Wee-wee-wee-wee-wee*   tickle underneath foot or
> *All the way home.*   under arm

Depending on how long you have to wait, you can go on and make up words to suit the situation:

> *This busy mother went to the bank*
> *This busy mother had to stand in line*
> *This little boy started to feel heavy*
> *This little boy started to squirm*
> *And this busy mother cried*
> *Oh good, oh good,*
> *The line is moving.*

Or you can recite, with real feeling and appropriate actions:

> *Slowly, slowly, very slowly,*
> *Creeps the garden snail. (Moves the line we're in)*
> *Slowly, slowly, very slowly,*
> *Up the wooden rail. (One step at a time).*
>
> *Quickly, quickly, very quickly*
> *Runs the little mouse.*
> *Quickly, quickly, very quickly*
> *Round about the house. (Scared the people away).*

You distract both your child and yourself, making the wait and the line seem shorter.

There are countless examples of nursery rhymes being universal and inter-generational. Merle and Gail's daughter Taryn have one in common, decades and continents apart. Both their parents used:

> *There was a little girl*
> *Who had a little curl,*
> *Right in the middle of her forehead.*

And when she was good,
She was very, very good,
But when she was bad
She was horrid!

Taryn had a mass of blonde curls and she and Merle had a "look" about them, bottom lip pushed out or something, that would alert their parents to the onset of a bad mood. They would immediately begin to recite. Sometimes, all it took to get a laugh and change of mood was the first line. It is still used with Taryn to acknowledge the onset of moodiness during the turbulence of adolescence.

Although Merle had sons, she too used this rhyme on occasion and she knows that Taryn will recite this rhyme as well when she is a mother. Rhymes passed on through the generations help bind families together, remind parents of how they behaved when they were children and, as such, put parenting into perspective.

Gail, like Merle, uses nursery rhymes when telling stories to first and second graders. At an appropriate time in her programme, when Gail feels the students need to stretch, she has them stand up and follow the actions for her "favourite" nursery rhyme.

Hickory Dickory Dock,	Clasp hands in front, move arms side to side like a pendulum
The mouse ran up the clock	Right hand fingers run up left arm
The clock struck one	Hold index finger high in the air
The mouse ran down	Fingers reverse journey down arm
Hickory Dickory Dock	Same as first movement
Tick Tock, Tick Tock, Tick Tock	Movement continues, voice becomes quiet.

After the first run through Gail explains "Unfortunately, my memory is not as good as it used to be. Perhaps you can help me." The students begin "Hickory Dickory Dock", but then Gail replaces *elephant* for *mouse*—they are dumbfounded. She asks them why they look so puzzled and is puzzled in turn when they tell her that she said *elephant*. This first line is repeated—with different ridiculous animals and never a mouse—until the students are laughing and shouting along. She then moves along to the second line:

> *Hickory Dickory Dock, the mouse ran up the clock,*
> *The clock struck fourteen—*
> *oh did I make a mistake again?*

The mouse has more problems on its return journey—it goes to Safeway, to MacDonald's, and to the library as the students, increasingly delighted, help this seemingly doddery old storyteller through the rhyme. By this time they've repeated it about twenty times, have laughed uproariously for about ten minutes and leave full of joy, repeating the rhyme for days afterward.

Years ago, around the time Velcro made its appearance, Merle found a pattern for a fabric Humpty Dumpty. She played around with the pattern and made the egg in three pieces, all held together with Velcro and with the arms and legs also attached this way. Merle and her sons would recite the rhyme:

> *Humpty Dumpty sat on a wall*
> *Humpty Dumpty had a great fall*

Craig and Scott would tug as Humpty tumbled, then gather up all his parts and "put him together again," shouting with great pride after

> *All the King's horse and all the King's men*
> *Couldn't put poor Humpty together again*

"*But Craig and Scott COULD!*" You cannot do more for self esteem than that! Humpty was also a great favourite of visiting friends.

Merle's family was fortunate because, shortly after they moved to Canada, Dennis Lee's book *Alligator Pie* was published. His rhymes and chants became family favourites and a strong memory for all three is a visit to their local bookstore to hear Lee recite his poems. Although Lee's collections are modern and, in many cases, celebrate Canada, they are also international as they have the same beat and exuberance of the traditional nursery rhymes. Lee's rhymes, with their pizzas, pumpernickels and washing machines, will be part of our grandchildren's heritage. He truly deserves to be known as "Father Gander."

In this age of political correctness, there has been much concern about perceived violence in nursery rhymes. One of Merle's strongest early memories is of her mid-thirties bachelor cousin Bill who, carrying her standing upright against his chest, would rush up and down the stairs in her grandmother's two-storied home reciting:

> *Goosey, goosey gander*
> *Whither shall I wander?*
> *Upstairs and downstairs*
> *And in my lady's chamber*
> *There I met an old man*
> *Who would not say his prayers*

When he got to:

> *I took him by the left leg*
> *And threw him down the stairs.*

Bill would hold Merle securely by the ankles and pretend to throw her down the stairs by swinging her gently through the air on the landing. Her mother told her he started this when she was around six months old and ended when she was around eighteen months. Although Merle held her breath every time he did this, she loved it, and can still remember that tingle of anticipation when Bill said "*prayers.*" She knew what was coming next and would stiffen herself ready for flight! Merle had a close and special relationship with Bill and always knew he would never let her down.

We often think some of the violence and anger we see coming from young people today is a result of them not being exposed to nursery rhymes and fairy tales. We all have to deal with our feelings, whether they be love, delight, pain, anger, sorrow or humour. Nursery rhymes allow parents and children to discuss these feelings as well as giving them choices for dealing with them. Children need to know anger can turn to rage, sorrow to delight, and that they are not alone in feeling the way they do. How many remember this childhood chant?

> *Sticks and stones*
> *May break my bones,*
> *But names will*
> *Never harm me.*

As adults we know this is not true and we need to instill in our children an appreciation for the power of words (and names). We must help them understand that words can hurt and harm just as surely as they can soothe and heal. Nursery rhymes empower children by allowing them to differentiate right from wrong. They also allow adults to keep the lines of communication wide open while at the same time giving notice that the world is not a perfect place.

Explore nursery rhymes with your babies and toddlers, as well as with older children. Experiment with actions to go with the words and rhythm and enjoy the interactions and imaginative play. Nursery rhymes offer a full range of involvement and activity, from rib-tickling, noisy laughter and bouncing, to soothing, calming and cuddling. This kind of play is the medium through which adult and child can express feelings and share experiences. Your children may not understand the language you are using but together with the actions there is a shared communication. At the same time as you are exercising their minds, you are also developing their small and large motor skills.

Lullabies and Songs are also important parenting tools. Lullabies are songs of slumber, songs of love. Even the word lullaby sounds soothing. Lull, from the middle English *lullen*, has counterparts in Swedish, *lulla* and Dutch, *lullen*. Lullabies are gleanings from folk history. Many are of unknown origin but mothers everywhere instinctively rock back and forth while serenading their babies. The rhythm and repetitiveness of the lullabies allows your voice, even if you don't have perfect pitch, tone or rhythm, to sound beautiful to babies and toddlers because they are sung by the people they love.

Not being musically adept, the songs Merle sang to the boys were the ones with simple tunes like:

Hush little baby, don't say a word
Papa's going to buy you a mockingbird
And if that mockingbird won't sing,
Papa's going to bring you a diamond ring.

If the diamond ring turns to brass
Papa's going to buy you a looking glass.
If that looking glass gets broke
Papa's going to buy you a billy-goat.

If the billy-goat won't pull
Papa's going to buy you a cart and bull.
If that cart and bull turn over,
Papa's going to buy you a dog named Rover.

If that dog named Rover won't bark,
Papa's going to buy you a horse and cart,
If that horse and cart fall down,
You'll still be the sweetest baby in town.

Hush little baby don't you cry.
Papa still loves you and so do I.

or

Hush-a-by baby on the treetop
When the wind blows, the cradle will rock;
When the bough breaks, the cradle will fall
Down will come baby, cradle and all

"Hush-a-by baby" is thought to have been written by a settler from the Mayflower who was intrigued with the way Indian women rocked their babies in birchbark cradle boards suspended from branches. One mother we know substitutes this last line "*Mother will catch you, cradle and all.*"

Michael Douglas's musical tribute honouring his father, actor Kirk Douglas, during the "1995 Kennedy Center Honors," was "Raisins and Almonds," an old Russian lullaby Kirk's immigrant mother had sung to him as a child.

> *To my little one's cradle in the night*
> *Comes a little goat snowy and white.*
> *The goat will trot to the market,*
> *While mother her watch does keep,*
> *Bringing back raisins and almonds.*
> *Sleep, my little one, sleep.*

Seeing the look of pure joy on Kirk Douglas' face as he listened to an elementary school choir singing the words his mother had sung decades before, reinforced not only the importance of lullabies in a child's life but also the power of memory. Kirk Douglas, although seated with thousands in the Kennedy Center, was far from there, hearing again his mother's soothing voice.

There are so many lullabies to choose from. They are sung at bedtime all over the world and everyone has their own special memories and favourites which are passed on from mother to child to child, again and again. The ones we choose to sing are very personal and depend to a large extent on our musical abilities. Lullabies and simple songs enable us to identify the similarity of songs known and loved around the world. We recognize the melody even when we don't understand the language.

Gail tells the story of visiting her husband's family in Holland when their daughters were quite young. There was a language problem, her husband's relatives spoke Dutch which she and her daughters did not understand. However, the ice was broken with the singing of "*Frere Jacques*"—in English, French and Dutch simultaneously.

Nursery rhymes and lullabies, however, are not only for the very young as the following two anecdotes demonstrate.

A woman who was caring for two toddlers came to a "Mother Goose" programme, where mothers, caregivers and toddlers recite nursery rhymes and listen to stories. On her second visit to the programme, she recounted to the group what had happened after her first visit the week before. That night, she had a run-in with her fifteen-year old daughter about not watching a late television show because she had a test at school the following day. Tempers flared and her daughter raced up to her room with the mother following, both shouting at one another. She opened her mouth to further reprimand her daughter, but said she suddenly remembered that nursery rhymes calmed you down and changed your voice tone. She found herself reciting "Pat a cake, Pat a cake, Baker's Man" out loud. When she had finished, quite calmed down, her daughter looked at her in delight and said "Oh mum, you are so strange!" All anger gone, they laughed and then reasonably discussed the television problem.

Another woman told of the time her eighteen-year-old daughter was coming out of anaesthetic after particularly gruelling surgery. When she asked her daughter what she could do for her, the request was simple, but unexpected. "Please, mum, stroke my head and sing 'Hush Little Baby' like you did long ago." Mother and daughter eased through what could have been a traumatic evening, both soothed and comforted by the words, the melody and the memories.

With the great leaps and bounds that have been made in technology in the past quarter century, there is security in knowing that the basic needs of babies and children today are not much different from earlier generations. Nursery rhymes and lullabies have never failed to soothe and heal. They are a rich and sustainable inheritance to pass on to your children. Pass them on with love and joy.

What is it that is not a shirt but is sewed; is not a tree but has leaves; and is not a person but yet talks sensibly?

(A Book)

NINE

TRADITIONAL FOLKLORE

When Gail tells stories in classes from kindergarten to grade three, she tells the tale of "The Three Wishes," a popular folktale in both France and Sweden that was brought to the new world with the settlers. The old woodcutter, after receiving three wishes along with a warning not to abuse his luck, immediately squanders his wishes with the help of his wife.

> *After eating their simple supper, the old woodcutter and his wife retire to the living room to further discuss how they should use their wishes—should they wish for wealth, power, children. They had just decided they would wait for morning to make their wishes known, when the woodcutter remembered a bottle of wine they had been saving for a celebration. "Surely, this is a time to celebrate," he said to his wife. "Do you know where the bottle is?" "Yes," replied his wife and she went off to fetch it. While he was waiting, the woodcutter thought to himself about his turn of luck—"I have always had a roof over my head and a wife who loves me, but now I can*

have anything I wish. Only thing is—right now I am a little hungry." And then, no longer to himself and without thought, the woodcutter continued aloud, "I wish I had a nice big piece of sausage to eat." And there on the floor was a large piece of fresh sausage.

When his wife returned to the room and saw the sausage on the floor, she was furious. "Oh, wife, I am so sorry. I just did not think!"

"That is always your problem, woodcutter—you never think." And she started to yell at him and yell at him, and the woodcutter became angrier and angrier. "I wish," he sputtered, "I wish that sausage was—stuck on the end of your—nose!"

And so it was! When the woodcutter looked at his wife, he saw two huge eyes, filled with tears, and a huge sausage attached to the end of her nose. There was only one thing he could do. He used the third wish to make the sausage disappear. The foolish woodcutter and his wife wasted all three of their wishes—and never even had a piece of sausage to eat!

Not only does this story amuse children (the thought of a sausage stuck on the end of a nose delights their imagination for some reason!), but it allows Gail to introduce them to some wonderful Canadian books based on the same theme of wishes and consequences. The three books usually introduced are *The Three and Many Wishes of Jason Reid* by Hazel Hutchins in which Jason uses his wishes creatively—his third wish is for three more wishes, Maryann Kovalski's story of *Frank and Zelda* and their restaurant, and the realistic tale of second-hand skates and the power of positive thinking (and skating practice) in *The Magic Hockey Skates* by Allen Morgan. These stories, plus a multitude of others based on other folktales, are appreciated in a different light once the reader is aware of their folkloric genesis. We can see that these old stories are still relevant today, retold in modern settings and situations to convey the same "truths" as have always been told.

One of the sad things we notice when we tell stories in schools is that many children are no longer familiar with a wide body of folktales. If they know any, the tales are always the same few: *Beauty and the Beast, Cinderella, Goldilocks and the Three Bears, Jack and the Beanstalk, The Little Mermaid, Little Red Riding Hood, The Princess and the Pea, Rapunzel, Rumpelstiltskin, Sleeping Beauty, Snow White, The Three Pigs* and *The Ugly Duckling.* These folktales come from collections of German tales collected by the Grimm brothers, French tales re-written for royalty by Perrault, and from the imagination of Hans Christian Andersen.

Of the large possible number of tales available to our children in books, it is regrettable to say that the same few tales are repeated over and over again, and most of these tales are the ones popularized by The Disney Studios. Parents and children, therefore, recognize a sanitized version of the tale. Few have any realization that the old tale the film was based upon tells a different story.

This familiarity with only a few of the world's folktales was vividly brought home to Gail while in a bookstore a few years ago. A very proud, new grandmother was browsing the shelves for a collection of fairy tales for the new child. Delighted with her enthusiasm, Gail, as a fellow customer, began to show her some of the best collections of fairy tales for young children. The woman looked at the contents and discarded any books containing tales that were not absolutely familiar to her. The collection she eventually purchased contained only eight fairy tales, all of them the most common tales and with that she was very happy. Before she left she thanked Gail for her help, looked at her very oddly and said, "If those other fairy tales were any good, I would have heard of them!"

As a storyteller, Gail does not tell the familiar stories, taking on the cause of making sure that the other tales, which are equally good, are also heard. As a parent, Gail made sure that her daughters never saw a movie based on a story, either traditional or literary, without hearing the story first. For years, the appropriate folktale, short story or novel was read before seeing the movie, and still the habit remains. Her family watches "Mystery" on PBS, reads the novels that are dramatized, and discusses the interpretations. Both Hugo's *Les Miserables* and Gaston Leroux's *Phantom of the Opera* became imperative reading when the stage productions reached Edmonton. The two fantasy readers in the family delight in finding a novel that is either based on an old tale or incorporates folktale motifs. Comparing the versions from the different media has become a family custom that generates plenty of discussion.

It also reaches beyond the family circle. In one of Esther's sign language classes the final assignment was retelling a folktale. The class was given a choice of four familiar tales, *Cinderella, The Three Pigs, The Three Bears*, and *Little Red Riding Hood* to sign. As the stories were discussed and practiced in class, Esther discovered the tales they were telling were not the versions with which she was familiar. "You're telling the Disney version," she would sign, and the class would watch bemused as she explained how the tale should be told. No Goldilocks in her version of *The Three Bears*, but an old woman! No woodcutter galloping to the rescue of Little Red, and plenty of blood flowing from maimed feet of the step-sisters in *Cinderella* as they tried to fit into the tiny glass slipper! The only story that did not show much change was *The Three Little Pigs*, the only one of the four folktales that was originally retold, in print, as a nursery tale for children.

While many people applaud these changes in the texts, remarking that the older versions are too violent or too sexist for children today, the justice and the logic inherent in those tales, for the most part, has been eradicated, leaving stories that are told for entertainment value only. We often sell our children short by assuming they are not able to understand what these age-old tales are telling them.

Even more lamentable is the number of children who insist the only stories they should listen to are "true." Truth has always been cloaked in parables and stories, as the most powerful religious leaders have always been aware, and this "truth" is understood by individual listeners within the realm of their own experience and understanding.

An old Jewish parable, which has been updated and told to modern audiences entitled "Sister Truth and Sister Story," points this out:

*Truth walked around town, naked and open to all that would
see him, but became increasingly forlorn as he realized
people would go out of their way to avoid him, crossing to the
other side of the street or turning around and walking in the
other direction. One day he went to Parable who was always
surrounded by large crowds of people. "Why," asked Truth,
"do people listen to you yet the same people go out of their
way to avoid me?" Parable replied, "Truth, look at me. I
proudly wear the finest clothes and jewels, my face and body
are annointed with perfume. When people see me, I make
them feel happy and secure. When people see you, the
naked Truth, it makes them uneasy and anxious. If you dress
like me, people will relax and will listen to you." Truth took
Parable's advice and dressed in a pleasing manner, and
when he walked the streets of the town, people were happy
to see him and listen to what he had to say.*

Our own children have always been aware of the underlying meaning of the tales we tell them but this awareness is not always
immediate. Many times they will come to us, long after they heard
the story, and make reference to it in conjunction with their own
behaviour or those of their friends. Like the African stories told to
Merle in her youth, all stories have a tendency to remain in the
background of our minds until we need them to help us understand
or articulate a problem or emotion.

"Tell me a story!"
"Once upon a time there was a. . . .

Telling stories in the family setting often involves the retelling of
traditional tales parents and grandparents remember from their own
childhood. These tales are part of the cultural heritage of the family.
Gail tells her children the Jewish tales that help define what it
means to be Jewish and that bring them closer to their ancestors.
Some of these tales were told by her family, others she has gone out
to find. She is drawn by all traditional tales, regardless of origin,
that celebrate cunning and wisdom over brute strength. Although

she tells stories to promote positive female role models for her daughters, not all of her favourite tales reflect this interest. She tells stories about all characters—female and male, positive and negative—because she wishes to acknowledge that the world is made up of *all* types of people.

One of these tales has a special significance for her. Several years ago her father was very ill and she did not know if he would survive. Fortunately, he did and one of his first outings was to come to a T.A.L.E.S. (The Alberta League Encouraging Storytelling) storytelling concert. The story she selected to tell at that time was this one.

> One day a young king decided that it was time for him to find a bride. Now, he did not care if she was tall or thin, blonde or dark, but he did want her to be intelligent. He decided to travel throughout his kingdom to find the most intelligent woman. He took off his royal garments and put on the clothes of a peasant. Suitably disguised he wandered up and down the roads and paths and through the villages and towns of his kingdom.
>
> As he was walking down one dusty road, the king met an old man and since they were going the same direction, asked, "Grandfather, where are you going?" The old man gave the name of a town and as that was the king's destination too, he asked if he could walk along with him. This was fine with the old man. They had not walked too far when the king turned to the older man and asked, "Grandfather, should I carry you or should you carry me?"
>
> "What a strange question," thought the old man, "he must be crazy. I am not going to answer him!" And he didn't; he just walked faster. The king did not say anything else either for a while until the two men came to a large field in which the heads of the ripening grain were beckoning them. "Grandfather." The king stopped and looked at the field. "Do you think that grain is already eaten or not?"
>
> "Already eaten or not! What kind of question is that? This man is truly crazy. I am not going to answer him." The older

man pursed his lips together tightly, lengthened his stride, and continued down the road. The king followed, silently, behind him. At long last they reached the walls of the city but could not enter until a funeral procession went by. "Grandfather, do you think the man inside the coffin is alive or dead?"

"He truly is mad! I am not going to bother with him a moment longer," thought the old man. Turning to the younger man he said, "Thank you for your hospitality. This is my town and I am going home now."

"Thank you for your hospitality, and don't forget to knock on your front door before you enter your home."

"Knock on my front door! Knock on my front door!" fumed the older man. "No one should tell me that! I do not need to knock on my own front door!" By the time he reached his house he was so upset that he stormed right through the doorway, throwing the door open with great force and knocking his daughter down onto the floor. "Oh, daughter, I am so sorry—I should have listened to what that young man said, but everything he said was such nonsense. I am so sorry."

"Father, slow down, calm yourself. What young man? What nonsense?"

Telling his daughter about the young man, the father explained she would never believe what the man had asked him.

"What, father?"

"First he asked, 'Grandfather, should I carry you or should you carry me?' Now, what kind of question is that? I am not so old that he had to carry me or he so young I need to carry him!"

"Oh, father. That is not what he meant at all. He wanted to know if he should tell you a story or you should tell him one. The journey is much shorter when you are listening to stories. It is as if the storyteller is carrying the listener."

"Perhaps that is what he meant," responded the old man grudgingly, "but that doesn't explain his next question. We walked past a field of grain and he asked me if I thought the

grain was already eaten or not! What kind of question is that?"

"Oh, father. What he was asking you was whether you thought the farmer had already sold the crop or not. If he had sold it and spent the money it would be as if the grain was already eaten."

"Oh, daughter. But you cannot explain his last question. We waited as a funeral passed by and he wanted to know if the man inside the coffin was alive or dead. Is that not nonsense?"

"Father, what he was asking you was whether or not the man inside the coffin had children. If the man had children then his line would live on, but if he had no children, then he was truly dead!"

"Oh, daughter, I have been so foolish. I must find that young man and apologize."

The old man went back through the town and found the king, still in his disguise. "I am so sorry, I understand now what you were asking me. Please come home for dinner."

"Who helped you understand?"

"My daughter. Please, please come this way."

The men arrived home just as the meal was ready. The young man sat at the table with the older man and his wife while their daughter brought in a platter filled with a roast chicken. Because the young man was a guest, she put the platter in front of him and asked him to carve the chicken. This he did, giving the wife the drumsticks, the daughter the wings, and the old man the head and neck. When the old man looked at his plate and saw the scrawny neck and head of the chicken, he became extremely angry. His face turned bright red and as he stood up to start yelling, his daughter gently put her hand on his shoulder. "Father, father. It is all right. The young man carved the chicken well. He gave the drumsticks to mother because she is always standing and working. He gave me the wings for one day soon I will marry and fly away from home. He gave you the head and neck because you are the head of the household. The rest he kept for himself because there was no one else to share it with."

When the king heard this he realized he had found the very clever woman he had been searching for. He asked the father if he could marry her, the father looked to his daughter and seeing her nod, replied yes. It was then the king threw off his disguise and the daughter discovered she was to become the queen. And that is the story of the daughter who was smarter than her father.

Gail always finishes her stories with the title as a signal the story is over, like the credits that roll across the screen after a movie or television show. This time, however, there was an added delight. As she finished saying the title, her father stood up in the audience and said, "It's not true, I am much smarter than she is!" At that moment she knew her father was really better.

If you are not familiar with many traditional tales, go to the public library and the 398.2 section (usually found in the children's area) and feast yourself on folktales from all over the world. *Folktales* are stories, told by the anonymous folk for generations, involving ordinary people having extra-ordinary adventures. A subset of folktales are the *fairytales* which include, as major characters, the wee folk and magic. Many of the tales referred to as fairy tales today have very little to do with the creatures of faerie. Little Red encounters a talking wolf, to be sure, but that is not that much out of the ordinary! We suggest a person should turn first to the folktales of their culture and heritage. While Gail was born in Canada, her ancestors came from Russia and many of the stories she tells also come from there. If those stories do not satisfy, then we suggest telling stories about a country you have visited or in which you have an interest. Several of Gail's favourite stories are from South East Asia where she spent several years as a young teacher. Not only does she tend to understand the characters in these tales, telling them brings back to life a part of her past. Merle tells stories she heard as a child. Many of her stories are African folktales, some of which she has been able to find in books, others she retells from memory. She also tells many traditional stories that her dad either told her or read to her.

Do not worry about memorizing the stories you find. Tell them in your own words. Storytelling is not memorization but bringing the "outline" of the action and characters alive to both yourself and the listener each time you tell the story. Don't fret if you are not telling the story the way it was written in the book you read. Only since the tales were first recorded in print were they frozen in development as well. Originally, each storyteller would imprint the tales told with her or his own personality and world view. This still happens to the tales told today by storytellers, both professionals and those within the family unit. It is the stories read from books that remain static, unchanging and, often, unrelated to the life and the needs of the listener.

One of the reasons picture book versions of folktales are so prolific is that folktales are in the public domain and therefore are not constrained by copyright issues. The stories become, in many cases, merely vehicles for the illustrator. One of the things that Gail stresses in her courses on storytelling is the careful selection of picture book folktales. Look not only to the pictures but to the language—is it poetic and rich in images that will feed the child's imagination and language development? Is the publisher and author/illustrator true to the source of the original story, stating where they found the tale? Are they true to the culture that tells the story? Does the picture book allow for interaction, not only with the text and the illustrations, but between the reader and listener? The choices for consumers and library users are enormous but, armed with a few ground rules (or questions), the task is manageable. In our bibliography, we have included only titles that meet these selection criteria.

Once the reader and child are familiar with the tale, the book can be put away and the tale can be told, with the family's own variations and adaptations, and it may become a household favourite. Tell the story from the child's point of view, or with the child as one of the characters, or change the setting (time and place) to one that is familiar to you and the listener. Children love to help you add imaginative details as they become willing participants in the creation of an original version of the traditional tale. It is no longer the story of *Goldilocks and the Three Bears*, but the story of *Brenda and the Three Little Gorillas*! The picture book, itself, can be read and looked at as a separate entity—a close friend—a work of artistic endeavour that tells a similar tale, but not necessarily your tale.

In order for these new versions to be developed, both parent and child must be familiar with the typical version. We suggest reading various versions of the same tale, looking at the different illustrations and the different ways the story may be told. Older children appreciate the parodies of folktales in picture books such as *The True Story of The Three Little Pigs, told by A. Wolf*, and *The Stinky Cheese Man and Other Fairly Stupid Tales*, both retold by Jon Scieszka. Younger children enjoy the tale of *Somebody and The Three Blairs* by Marilyn Tolhurst. By reading these creative retellings, along with the traditional versions, children soon realize that the stories can be played with and that there is not one, and one only, "correct" version. This is a lesson that is sometimes difficult for university students as they have not been exposed to the wide variety of folktales and versions before.

Another significant area of the library is the 292 section which houses myths and legends from around the world. Knowledge about mythology is essential for the child's rounded development. One of the most difficult discussions for some students is the one on mythology. The major problem is the popular meaning that has become associated with the word "myth." To many it means a falsehood, and this misunderstanding of the word is kept in the foreground by the press who write "Ten Common Myths about . . ." when they are really discussing misconceptions. *Myths* are not misrepresentations or fabrications but are, by definition, the sacred stories of a people; the stories that define the religious truths that comprise their belief systems. When referring to the myths in the Bible, we are not being derogatory but rather are speaking of the stories contained within the covers of that very powerful book of beliefs. Every religious culture maintains its own mythology, its own set of sacred tales that deserve the respect we feel our own beliefs should be accorded.

Children should be familiar with the myths that comprise their own background, but they should also be acquainted with those of others. This is one road to human understanding and world peace. But it is also more than that. The classic myths of the Greeks and Romans and the more earthy myths of the Norse are reflected daily in our North American culture and language. The days of the week and the names of the months reflect mythic origins. For example, the first month of the year was dedicated by the Romans to their two-faced god, Janus, because one face could look forward to the new year, while the other face could look back on the year just completed. Additional examples are discussed in the following chapter on folklore in popular culture.

While it is not essential to know the origins of these words in order to communicate effectively, it does enhance our quality of life. The ancient myths helped to provide answers to questions about nature that the early inhabitants observed but could not understand. The resulting *mythos* (or stories) as the Greeks labelled them, told of the constellations, the flora and fauna, and the origins of the world. Whether the explanations are the ones prescribed in your family belief system or not, these myths are part of the universal exploration of life and can be told while walking through the backyard or on a trip through a grocery store. Children will remember which flower is a daisy if they are told the short story about its name and how it came directly from the Old English phrase, "day's eye" to explain the flower opening in the morning with the rising sun, and closing again at night with the fall of the sunshine.

The forget-me-not is explained by one old German folk legend.

> *A man, following the trail of a beautiful blue flower, was led down through mountain paths to a cave. Inside the cave he found immense towers of gold and silver, treasures beyond contemplation. While standing there in awe, a lovely woman appeared before him and counselled him to "Forget not the best." He paid no attention to her warning, and taking only the gold and jewels, he left the little blue flower behind. As he left the cave, a rock slide crushed the man and closed the cave forever, burying the treasure for all time.*

Another myth tells of a time when God was naming all the plants and a little blue flower could not remember its name. Finally God whispered to it, "Forget me not—that is your name."

A few years ago, Gail, Peter, their two daughters, and Gail's brother piled into the family car and traveled through the night to attend a family gathering in Winnipeg. They left Edmonton after supper and drove steadily until they reached their destination, stopping only for gas and coffee along the route. The journey was not, in itself, all that memorable (except for the realization that their daughters were no longer small children and they took up as much space as an adult!) but Gail did come away with a powerful resolve to take more notice of our sky. The trip through the prairies on a clear fall night unfolded a sky that told numerous stories. Unfortunately, only a few fragments of the majority of these tales could be recalled. The ancient civilizations knew the power of the sky and created stories that helped to express their wonder and amazement at the sight. Just recently we were attending a gathering at a home on the outskirts of St. Albert, just outside Edmonton. It was April and, again, the sky was clear. A telephone call alerted us to the show that Mother Nature was putting on display and we filed out to the deck to watch the Northern Lights dance in all their splendour. Several people had come from other parts of the world and had never seen the Aurora Borealis. The sight was something they would never forget. Today, many of us reside in cities, away from the wide open vistas of the night sky and we forget about the stars and the stories that are attached to them. Sit out in the back yard—hopefully the city lights will not lessen the impact—and celebrate, through story, the wonders and lessons of nature.

On a tour through the art galleries in Italy, Gail also realized that the ancient myths have provided the inspiration for many of the world's masterpieces. As she and her family made their way slowly through the paintings, statues and fountains, Gail was reminded again and again of the stories and mythical characters that kept appearing and she told her family snatches of the stories while standing in the galleries.

Legends are stories that tell of a more recent time, and of characters who may have resided in historical time like William Tell, Robin Hood, and King Arthur and the Knights of the Round

Table. Legends also include stories that explain the naming of an area or some feature of geography. These local legends repeat the same themes in various localities. Numerous lovers' leap stories are told about cliffs and waterfalls in various locations in North America, Japan and Europe. One of the most renowned local legends has given its name to consumer products as well as a common saying. This is the legend from Coventry, England, and the famous ride of Lady Godiva.

> *In a desperate attempt to get her husband to reduce taxes, Lady Godiva agreed to accomplish a deed that her husband suggested in jest. She would ride naked through the town. To protect her modesty, she asked the townspeople to lock themselves in their homes with their windows shuttered during her ride. They all agreed, but one tailor, named Tom, could not resist taking a peep at her as she rode past. Tom was immediately struck blind and his action forever celebrated in the term "Peeping Tom"!*

Western Canadian legends are told of the early settlers and cowboys, early politicians and newspaper reporters who left their mark in history. Some of these stories are based on true events but, with the passage of time, have become coloured and embellished by the storytellers. When we go camping in the Rocky Mountains, we tell tales of the legendary explorers who first travelled the paths and rivers we are travelling now. We may not be standing exactly where those earlier travellers stood, but we feel the connection to the past and to their courage and stubbornness. In awe of the majestic peaks, we are also in awe of the people who left their names (as well as those who remain unknown) in the wilderness.

The following brief historical notes illuminate the naming of Jasper townsite and Jasper National Park, the Yellowhead Highway and Mt. Fryatt in Jasper National Park, demonstrating various sources and stories behind the names.

> *In 1813, the North West Company built a supply depot on Brule Lake and called it Jasper House after company clerk*

Jasper Hawes. Later, when the site was moved to the present location of Jasper, Alberta, the name moved as well. Also in the early 1800s, an Iroquois trader, Pierre Bostonnais, guided men of the Hudson Bay Company through the northern Rocky Mountains. His light-coloured hair resulted in the nick name "Tete Jaune" or "Yellowhead." A major highway across western Canada, the Yellowhead, and the town of Tete Jaune Cache on the Yellowhead High-way, still reflect his guiding prowess (and his hair-colouring). In more recent history, a mountain peak, Mt. Fryatt, was named in honour of Captain Charles Fryatt who, during World War I, rescued and transported Allied soldiers across the English Channel in his boat, The Brussels. Fryatt was later captured and executed for attempting to ram a U-boat.

If we don't know the story behind something and can not find it, we often make up our own, creating continuity with the past and the future because those tales also become part of our family history. "Remember when we went climbing and Dad told the story of . . .?"

Along with the legends that help to form our land and our understanding of it are the *tall tales*, the tales of exaggeration—not lies—that were the survival tools of a frontier land. These tales, of winters so cold words froze and had to be thawed out before the conversation could continue, have been told for centuries but were so well adapted to the western provinces and states that they became identified with cowboys, farmers, blacksmiths, railroad men, lumbermen, and their gathering places.

In the early history of Alberta settlement, there was one man who moved so often that whenever a large wagon came anywhere near his house, his chickens all marched up, fell on their backs and crossed their legs, ready to be tied up and carried to the next stopping place.

Livestock owners at that time were oblivious to property lines, letting their animals forage for food. And so, not too far from that man's house:

> *A hungry hog came upon a crew working with dynamite to clear some tree stumps off the railroad right-of-way. No one took any notice of the hog—not even when he gobbled up a stick of dynamite, percussion cap and all. He had barely left the area when the hog paid the price of pilferage: the crew set off the blasting charge igniting the dynamite the pig had swallowed. When the debris settled, the astonished crew found two smoked hams, a generous supply of pork chops and some barbecued ribs!*

These tales of exaggeration are told in a matter-of-fact manner, as the absolute truth! In the West's early history, these tales were told by men to entertain themselves but also to differentiate the "greenhorns" from the established residents. Today, we usually identify these types of stories with fishermen and the "big one that got away."

One of the easiest methods for children to become comfortable in telling stories is to encourage them to start with other forms of folklore, particularly riddles, jokes and jump rope rhymes.

> *Knock, knock.*
> *Who's there?*
> *Banana.*
> *Banana who?*
> *Knock, knock.*
> *Who's there?*
> *Banana.*
> *Banana who?*
> *Knock, knock.*
> *Who's there?*
> *Banana.*
> *Banana who?*
> *Knock, knock.*
> *Who's there?*
> *Orange.*
> *Orange who?*
> *"Orange-cha" glad I didn't say Banana?*

Children love to set *riddles* that celebrate their exploration of the sound and meaning of language. As parents we may tire (just a little) as we are asked another (or the same) "knock-knock" joke-riddle, but we bravely respond, "Who's there?"

Jokes and riddles are part of folklore, part of the heritage of the past when families enjoyed word games to help pass the time while engaged in survival pursuits that were repetitive and boring. Early riddles and jokes were often based on the Bible, the only reading material in many pioneer homes. Many of the "true riddles" (those that can be answered through reason) were based on observations of nature, weather patterns, and animal behaviour.

> *The more you feed it*
> *The more it'll grow high,*
> *But if you give it water,*
> *Then it'll go and die.*
> *What is it?*   (Fire)

As we respond to the riddles and jokes "invented" and told by our children, we are encouraging them in an exploration of language as well as other important aspects of development. Our publisher, Gary Whyte tells of his youngest son, Cory, a five-year-old who loves to make up his own riddles. Cory's proud father explains: "Usually his riddles are not funny and make no sense whatsoever. But we laugh all the same and the glow in Cory's eyes and the sense of pride and excitement—and self-worth—are a wonder to behold!"

All cultures have riddles and jokes and, in several, the answering of a riddle forms the basis of many folk tales as a method of teaching critical thinking skills. Many of the stories surrounding the historical King Solomon are tales of him demonstrating his wisdom by solving a question/riddle set before him.

Jokes constitute the most common type of folklore told today. Children begin very young, playing with sounds, rhymes and non-sense words to make jokes and riddles they find outrageously funny. They graduate to riddle-jokes and sick-jokes as they grow older. As parents, one listens to countless jokes that are really not "funny" at all. As children grow older, they begin telling "insider" jokes, ones they feel their old parents would never understand in a hundred years. They then begin experimenting with "dirty" jokes and continue on by entertaining peers and family members with the types of jokes that are most suitable and appropriate for the audience and occasion. Jokes travel in cycles and reappear, sometimes disguised as a new "type" of joke, in each generation. Thus, the new jokes that children are telling are often old jokes to the older audiences. Jokes are also told as a defense mechanism when things appear to be going out of control. Therefore, disaster jokes are cracked almost simultaneously with the disastrous occurrence. In order for people to keep their perspective, they must be able to laugh or respond in some way. Jokes also reflect peoples' attitudes towards minorities. One interesting exercise for Gail's family was to compare the "Newfie" jokes told here in Alberta with the types of jokes told in other geographical locations around the world. The content of the jokes was the same, the "actor" always reflected the scapegoat for each individual culture. Thus in the Netherlands, they found the same "Newfie" jokes told about people from Belgium.

In today's political climate, jokes, particularly ethnic jokes, are highly frowned upon as these jokes promote and reinforce the stereotypes minority groups are always fighting. While we do not believe in passing on these negative and harmful stereotypes, it is important to note the historical links between the types of jokes being told and the overall values and attitudes of the community.

Traditional folklore—be it stories or brief kernels of wisdom (proverbs, pithy sayings and weather predictions), or humourous responses to our world (jokes and riddles)—is a necessary component of anyone's education. Society constantly builds on past observations to learn from history, scientific discoveries and the wisdom of the folk.

Tell your children the stories and jokes you heard as a child, and listen to the stories and jokes circulating today. Chances are you will hear numerous similarities and connections between your childhood and that of your children.

If you feel overwhelmed by the "task" of finding tales you feel comfortable telling, turn to our suggestions and those that are on your library shelf. Explore, play, and connect members of your family with the appropriate "lore" of your folk.

While sitting outside and admiring the stars twinkling high above you, make your wish, turn to the person beside you, and tell this "noodle tale" from Japan.

> *One night an old man saw a young man waving a long bamboo pole about in the temple garden. "What are you doing?" asked the older man. "I am trying to get a star down from the sky, but I am unable to hit one." "How foolish you are," the old man responded angrily. "Your pole is not long enough. Take it up to the roof and try from there!"*

Who knows what you will hear in return!

It belongs to all of us, this mood of once upon a time. . . .

T.J. Bjorn

TEN

FOLKLORE IN POPULAR CULTURE

A cartoon in the "Saturday Comics" demonstrates the interweaving of traditional folklore in our everyday popular culture. Piraro, creator of the cartoon *Bizarro*, parodied the tale of *Snow White* by showing a scene (complete with two attendant blue birds) that could have stepped right out of the Disney Studios version of the tale. In the cartoon, the young girl, dressed in the immediately recognizable attire of this film heroine, is in the process of selecting one of the scarves hanging on pegs on the wall while looking at herself in the mirror. She rejects the scarf because, as she states, it makes her look *dopey*. To make sure every viewer immediately understands the parody, Piraro included a framed title within the cartoon: *Snow White and the Seven Scarves*. A quick glance back at the pegs—yes, there are seven different scarves. An additional clue to the origin of the parody is in the use of the word *Dopey*, one of the names given by Disney Studios to the dwarves. (Only in the Disney version do these characters have individual names.)

This is a prime example of folklore in popular culture. Many people have a preconceived notion that folklore is something old and not particularly relevant in our modern technical society. However, when we turn to the media we are bombarded by folklore, in everything from brand names and jingles, movie and television plots to words in the English language. Gail has been introducing students and educators to this concept for six years, and continually discovers new material to discuss. When preparing this chapter she turned to several sections of the Edmonton *Yellow Pages* and quickly found numerous examples of brand names with a direct reference to the mythology and folktales of our ancestors.

Those who need help with noisy cars can turn to *Midas* muffler shops for assistance. Midas was a legendary king in Greek mythology whose every touch turned items to gold, to his eventual dismay. Gail is quite sure this is not exactly the message the *Midas* company wishes to promote; they probably hope the general public are familiar with just the first part of the legend, the "golden touch." She also located *Hansel and Gretel* children's clothing stores, which take the name from the tale of the two children left in the woods and their courageous escape from danger. *Sweeping Beauties* maid service provides a pun on the title of the folktale "Sleeping Beauty" and *Noah's Ark Pet Centre* connects with a direct allusion to a story from the Bible. Other folkloric allusions include *Jack & Jill* children's clothing stores, *Wizard* T-shirts, *Café Shangri-la* and *Shangri-la Restaurant*, *Humpty's*, *Egg Me On*, *The Daily Grind Coffee House* and the *Blue Willow Restaurant*.

Jack and Jill are two familiar names in the world of nursery rhymes that consumers would immediately connect to products for young children. Wizards are famous folklore characters that are popular today in everything from fantasy novels to computer games and T-shirt outlets. Shangri-la, a famous place of the imagination, was introduced to readers in 1933 through the novel *Lost Horizon* by James Hilton. It became even more popular when American president F.D. Roosevelt used the term for his mountain refuge in Maryland. Shangri-la also referred to the "secret" military base used in 1942 for the American air raid on Tokyo. Countless restaurants, specializing in oriental food, use an association with this "exotic" place to intrigue customers. A restaurant chain, *Humpty's*, offers a menu consisting of, possibly, only broken eggs. Both *Egg*

Me On and *The Daily Grind Coffee House* are based on popular sayings: "to egg on" meaning to incite someone to action, and "daily grind" which usually refers to everyday routine, used here as a pun for the name of a coffee house.

The *Blue Willow Restaurant* is an extremely nostalgic name for Gail. Her parents owned a gift and jewellery store in Viking, Alberta and would travel to Edmonton to purchase their wares from travelling salesmen who set up shop at the Hotel MacDonald. Some of her sharpest memories are of her brother and herself playing in and around that grand hotel, and of the family going out to the *Blue Willow Restaurant* for lunch. Crossing the arched bridge inside the restaurant to get to the tables always seemed to be a magical voyage into a world filled with wonder. As she grew older she realized the Blue Willow china pattern played an important role in the settlement of several frontiers, particularly western Canada and South Africa. The early pioneers had their special dishes (Gail still has one plate of her grandmother's set) and the Blue Willow pattern was one of the most common ones. When books were at a premium, parents and grandparents would tell the romantic story depicted on the plates.

A few years ago, when telling stories in a retirement home, one woman asked if we knew that story—her mother had always told it to her on special occasions when the best dishes were brought out. Decades had passed and she remembered the dishes and the emotion, but she could not remember all the details of the story—could we tell it? Of course we could.

Although people assumed the pattern and story originated in China, this was not the case: the only resemblance to any Chinese porcelain pattern is the blue and white colouring. The story has no Chinese counterpart. This verse, found in many nursery rhyme collections, was the genesis of the story.

> *Two pigeons flying high,*
> *Chinese vessel sailing by.*
> *Weeping willow hanging o'er,*
> *Bridge with three men, if not four.*
> *Chinese mansion here it stands,*

Seems to cover all the land.
Apple tree with apples on,
And a pretty fence to hang my song.

In 1849, *The Family Friend*, a Victorian magazine, published a tragic love story alleged to be the basis for the Willow pattern which was introduced in Shropshire around 1780. This was probably the most successful marketing strategy of all time; nearly one hundred and fifty years later, the Blue Willow pattern is still being sold and the story is still being told.

The story is long and involved but here is a summary.

Long, long ago, a rich but tyrannical mandarin built a magnificent two-story house on an island. The house was surrounded by landscaped gardens, valuable trees and a high wall. A river flowed through the gardens and over an arching bridge.

After his wife's death, the mandarin retired to this house along with his daughter, Koong-se and his calligrapher Chang. Koong-se and Chang fell in love, but knowing such a union would never be allowed, they were as discreet as could be. However, her father soon discovered they were meeting, banished Chang from the estate and promised his daughter in marriage to an elderly rich duke. The ceremony was to be held when the peach tree blossomed.

Imprisoned in her father's mansion with no chance of contacting Chang, Koong-se was about to give up hope when she noticed a coconut shell floating on the river. She retrieved it and discovered a calligraphed poem from Chang: when the willow blossoms fall and the peach starts to blossom he would commit suicide. She sent the coconut shell back with a message begging him to come for her just before the willow blossoms fell.

This occurred on the evening the pre-nuptials began. A beggar came for alms. When the party was in full swing, the beggar revealed himself to Koong-se as Chang, ready to take her away with him. Taking her groom's gift of jewels, they

> *made their escape. The mandarin caught sight of the fleeing lovers and chased them over the bridge.*
>
> *The lovers eluded him and Koong-se's maid hid them in her humble home where they were married. The mandarin posted a reward for their capture and the house was surrounded. The faithful maid delayed the searchers long enough for the lovers to escape in a small rowboat with the jewels.*
>
> *They had a rough and terrifying journey, surviving by their wits, and eventually reached a small island where they lived happily for some time. The spurned duke, seeking revenge, attacked the island with an army and Chang was killed. A distraught Koong-se set their home on fire and perished in the blaze. Koong-se and Chang were transformed into the two immortal doves seen flying above the peach tree* (on the plates).

Merle's grandmother managed to get Merle to eat just about anything so she could clear the plate and hear the story. Merle believed if her grandmother could not see the pictures, she would not remember how to tell the story.

We have a fascination with the modern adaptation of folklore and how each historical era builds on the tales and wisdom of the elders to fashion innovative versions that have relevancy to new generations. Because of this, one of Gail's favorite assignments for storytelling students is to locate three items of folklore in popular culture. Before they can do this, they must be familiar with the three different types of culture in our society.

Popular culture is created by identifiable "authors" and makes up our novels, television shows, films, comics, newspapers, magazines, brand names, advertisements and popular music. It is different from both elite culture and folk culture in scope and in perceived importance within the education system.

Elite culture, the world of symphony, theatre, classic literature and music, is the creation of known "authors" as are the works of popular culture but, unlike popular culture, is considered worthwhile for inclusion in schools.

Folk culture, on the other hand, includes the lore, the sayings and the stories of "anonymous" people, and is often thought of as unworthy of our modern, urban, and technological society.

So, while western society studies the elite culture and is entertained by the popular culture, the folk culture is employed by advertisers, politicians and other salespeople to help sell a product or an idea or to convey a "truth" without the need for a great deal of additional explanation. Folk culture, or folklore, represents the voice of the people—the folk—and by being aware of folklore around us, we become more aware of our own roots, directions and futures.

Gail's students always complain that this assignment will be too difficult. How will they ever find three such items? Where should they look? Why do the silly assignment anyway? After being assured that it really is not impossible, they are set loose and, lo and behold, every time, the students discover that their major problem is deciding which three of the many examples they have found should be used in their paper! They turn to the *Yellow Pages*, their television screens, their favourite song lyrics, the newspapers and cartoons, and conversations with their friends and family for examples. Once they realize what they are looking for, the students have no problem recognizing the folkloric content. What always amazes them is the virtual lack of duplication between their examples and those of their classmates. In a period of a few weeks almost ninety examples of folklore can easily be found by thirty students. Both of Gail's daughters had a similar assignment in Grade 10 English classes. To the horror of the university students, the high school assignment was more defined and difficult, asking for *ten* examples of *mythology* in popular culture, rather than the entire realm of folklore.

The overall consensus of the students is that they were never aware of the vast amount of folklore surrounding them in their daily life and that the simple fact of "stopping to look" has opened their eyes to the ways in which our society subconsciously absorbs and understands images and messages.

You may wonder, in a book about telling stories in the family, why we are spending considerable space on such a topic. As parents, we feel it is important that our children know not only the stories behind their own names but that they should know the backgrounds alluded to in their immediate surroundings. Recognizing the folklore content of the novels, films and television programmes we read and watch enhances our understanding of the storyline. After all, these did not just fall into the script by accident!

By being familiar with the myths, legends and folktales that have lent their titles and characters to modern businesses and mass communication, children are better equipped to understand what is being conveyed to them by popular culture. This is not an overwhelming task. The creators of popular culture only use the folklore they assume will be familiar to their target audiences. Less then a dozen folktales are referred to over and over again. And of these, only certain aspects of the tales are used: *Sleeping Beauty* and the kissing prince who woke her up, the basket of goodies of *Little Red Riding Hood*, the climb to the giant's castle in *Jack and the Beanstalk*, *Snow White* and the magic mirror, *Rumplestiltskin* and the guessing of names, *Hansel and Gretel* and the oven, *The Frog Prince* and the ball in the well, and *The Three Little Pigs* with their "chinney-chin-chins" and the wolf's huffing and puffing. *Cinderella* and *Beauty and the Beast* are the two most common folktales used by advertisers. Certain elements are used over and over again: the royal ball (dance) and the coach and pumpkin escapade, and the transformation of the Beast into something quite beautiful by the power of love (or a good face cream).

Because we are beset by advertisements at an early age through the magic of television, we should realize that many of the products sound familiar and necessary because of the unconscious recognition we have with the tales locked in our memories. The familiar ring of the folk material convinces the consumer that the product too is familiar and will stand the test of time. Giants are no longer considered frightening, rather they are good overlords for our vegetables (*Green Giant*). Genies help us to clean our households (*Mr. Clean*) and the legendary Robin Hood helps us to be successful bakers (*Robin Hood Flour*).

Often it is not a particular tale that is alluded to within popular culture, but the idea of "living happily ever after" or the idea of "fairy godmothers" and "waiting for the prince to come" that is behind the media message. Products which have a long affiliation with a character from folklore often lose that association in time because of society's unfamiliarity with the traditional literature. Few people are aware that Mercury, the Roman messenger god of science and commerce as well as travellers and thieves, is the figure in the logo of *FTD* flower delivery service, or that the *Mercury* automobile is blessed with the name of the god of travellers. The planet and the liquid metal associated with thermometers were also named as an association with this god's attributes and responsibilities. While on the subject of cars, look to Pontiac's *Phoenix* (the bird who rises from the ashes), Ford's *Taurus* (the bull and the second sign of the zodiac and, like all of the astrological signs, based on folklore), plus the *Sunbird*, the *Legend* and the *Thunderbird*.

Legendary qualities are often "loaned" to sports teams through their names. The *Argonauts*, in Greek mythology, were the sailors of the galley "Argos" who sailed with Jason on his search for the golden fleece. Argos, in the Greek language, means swift. The Canadian football team, the *Toronto Argonauts*, are on their "swift" quest each season for the golden fleece of the Canadian Football League: the Grey Cup.

One concern of parents is the selection of appropriate folk tales and myths for their children. Our response is to point parents in the direction of the nursery rhymes, folk tales, legends and myths that play a large role in our popular culture. It is our firm belief that children and consumers should be familiar with these and other folktales and not just the modern retellings that permeate western society. The family could explore numerous variants of *Cinderella* (or any of the folktales mentioned above) through picture books and story collections at the local library to see how many of the elements of these tales show up almost daily in our mass media. Families can base discussions on how they identify with the characters.

Sometimes this identification comes from a surprising source.

We know two sisters who have worked together for years and we spend a great deal of time listening to these elderly women telling us of their childhood and their Cree culture.

Just recently they were joined, in their work, by a third sister,
the youngest in a large family. She introduced herself as the
Cinderella of the family: the one who had to do ALL the work!
As her sisters laughed with her, they explained she was the
spoiled one, although they all had to work hard. We realized
that, although they grew up immersed in their own native
culture, they adopted folklore motifs from the broader culture
as well and assumed we would know exactly what they were
talking about with that one comment.

So, our first answer to these parents is to be aware of the stories referred to in the mass media and make it their responsibility that their children know these tales. Look to the media as a story directory.

The words we speak and write are often based on folklore as well. As mentioned in an earlier chapter, we take for granted the names of the days of the week and the months of the year, but few of us realize that the majority of them are based on mythology. Other adjectives, adverbs, nouns, verbs and figures of speech also have their roots in ancient tales. For example, scientific terminology is heavily weighted in mythology. Chemical elements reminded their discoverers of mythical beings, so cobalt is named after the *kobalts* of German folklore who were in the habit of tricking people in their underworld environment. It was named because the element itself "tricked" the miners attempting to bring it to the surface. Iridium is named after *Iris*, the Greek goddess of the rainbow, because of the colours inherent in the compound. The Norse god of Thunder, *Thor*, gave his name to the element thorium because of its heavy radioactive nature.

Animal and plant classification systems and names reflect the wider world of folklore. Spiders are known as *Arachnida*, named after *Arachne* and her misguided weaving contest with the Greek goddess *Athena*.

Arachne, an extremely talented weaver, was very proud of
her accomplishments. She bragged she was a better weaver
than even the goddess of wisdom and the arts and sciences.
The angry goddess, Athena herself, appeared in the guise of

an old woman at Arachne's door. When she could not con-
vince Arachne of her superior talent, Athena threw off her
disguise and challenged the young weaver to a contest.
Although fearful of the angry goddess, Arachne was con-
vinced of her proficiency, and she quickly and skillfully wove
into her tapestry countless stories of the errors and misdeeds
of the gods. This further angered the goddess who tore
Arachne's work into a web of tatters. Devastated by this
action and the strength of Athena's displeasure, Arachne
hung herself in grief. A calmer Athena then transformed
Arachne into a spider so she could continue to weave.

Natural phenomena have also been explained through the use of ancient myths and these tales live on with the continued use of these terms. For example, *Echo and Narcissus*'s story gave rise to the naming of the narcissus flower as well as the echo in empty rooms and in the mountains. The story of the infatuated nymph and hunter is found in almost every collection of Greek myths and is taught in upper elementary classes.

Newspapers are always utilizing folklore to grab attention for their news stories. Those who write newspaper headlines (not necessarily the same ones who wrote the news articles) use familiar sayings, proverbs and quotations as well as nursery rhymes as a capsule invitation to the content of the article. Often the familiar is cleverly twisted by these writers to stop the browsers in their tracks. Movies and television programmes also borrow from folklore to tell their stories. *Star Wars* is based on the structure of traditional folktales and hero myths: a young boy leaves home on a quest to find his own identity. Some old tales are continually being reworked for the visual media such as the characters of the legendary Sherwood Forest in the movie *Robin Hood, Prince of Thieves* and *Beauty and the Beast* in the television series and movie of the same name.

A very important visual interpreter of folklore themes and tales are cartoons. Gary Larson of *Far Side* fame used folkloric themes liberally as do many of the cartoonists for the *New Yorker* magazine. Cartoon strips such as "One Big Happy" employ folktales to establish rapport with the readers. We often refer to these cartoons, and others, when showing the influence of folklore on popular culture. Many of our children's comic book heroes are also based on folklore characters brought to life once more. *Superman*, *Thor*, and *Spiderman* are three we remember as children; all have antecedents in cultural myths.

An early hobby in which Gail still retains some interest is stamp collecting. Because both her mother and brother collected Canadian stamps, she looked to other countries and interests. Early on she discovered that many of the East European countries issued stamps based on the folktales of their people. In today's world of specialization, interest groups have developed and one of these in the postage stamp world is The American Topical Association, a non-profit educational organization of topical stamp collectors, which publishes handbooks on various topics. One of these is "Fairy Tales and Folk Tales on Stamps" which lists all the stamps that depict folklore. In 1992, Canada Post Corporation issued four stamps of Canadian folklore, and a booklet containing the four tales, "with vivid illustrations, which parents and children can enjoy together." Another souvenir edition of stamps, on Canadian legendary creatures, was issued at the same time. Unfortunately, the stamps were for collectors only and have not had a wide circulation or impact on Canadian letter writers.

Our traditional holidays are filled with elements of folklore. Try thinking of Valentine's Day without the cute little "Cupid" shooting arrows of love, if not at people, then at the characters on the greeting cards that appear in the shops. *Cupid*, the god of love in Roman mythology, has been transformed, through time and illustrations in Valentine greeting cards, from a handsome deity to a chubby cherub with wings. His traditional purpose, however, has not changed as much.

Two important folk creations which are identified with traditional holiday seasons are *Santa Claus* (loosely based on the historical St. Nicholas) and the *Easter Bunny*. Recent outcry has remarked that Canadians have lost sight of the religious meaning of these holidays and have infused too much importance on consumerism and the folklore characters created by the people. In the Netherlands, they returned to a secular celebration, St. Nicholas Day on December 6, when gift giving is the order of the day, and the religious celebration of Christmas on December 25. They were dissatisfied with combining the two aspects of the modern Christmas as it is held in other parts of the world. Oddly enough, one of the Christmas cards we received from the Netherlands this year, pictured a jolly, chubby Santa Claus rather than the tall, stately, traditional St. Nicholas.

This is always an interesting discussion for Gail. Growing up Jewish on the Alberta prairie provided her with a "detachment" from the holiday.

I did not celebrate any aspect of Christmas until I married my non-Jewish spouse, although I participated in school Christmas concerts and was exposed to the various stories and images of the season. Santa Claus was someone who brought gifts to the other kids. He brought me an orange! Actually, I have two vivid images of Christmas when I was growing up. The first image was of the gift-giving Santa, both the one who appeared at the movie theatre and gave us each a Christmas orange, and the one who was responsible for the "miraculous" appearance of a mesh bag of goodies hanging on our front door each Christmas morning. I was much older when I discovered the identity of that second Santa. I bless our next door neighbour, the school principal, for realizing, that of all the children in school, we would have no gifts each season. (Hanukkah gift-giving is a recent innovation that was probably spurred by others who shared my experience).

My second childhood image of Christmas is related to this realization. It is one of isolation; Christmas was always the loneliest time of the year, with Easter a close second. All our neighbours and friends were involved with holiday preparations and expectations and their days were filled with visits from relatives and with excitement. For us, there wasn't even anything good on television! This early experience has had a profound effect on the way I view the Christmas celebration today with my own children and Peter's family. The importance of the folklore and traditions surrounding Christmas was brought home to me very clearly the year I celebrated the holiday in Australia. Our friends and neighbours made a traditional Christmas meal with roast turkey and mashed yams and served it to us in an over-heated house at the height of their summer hot spell.

Other aspects of our modern Christmas celebration based on folklore include the use of evergreens, holly and mistletoe to decorate our homes, the decorated Christmas tree and the use of candles and lights to brighten the winter scene. Easter, too, is filled with folklore of earlier times from the Hot-cross buns to decorated eggs.

As storytellers, we are more attuned to the folklore and traditions of another holiday season: Halloween. This celebration is filled with folklore characters from various cultures: witches, vampires, ghosts, black cats, and princesses. It is also filled with stories of "Trick or Treat" pranks and activities that are not considered either "proper" or "safe" today. Granted there are not a lot of outhouses to tip over anymore but the community spirit that united us when we were growing up no longer seems to be a part of Halloween. When Gail was growing up in rural Alberta, it was the one time of the year the children realized teachers were actually human—several of them dressed up and went along with their young neighbours on their routes while others stayed at home and transformed their homes and yards to promise scary and exciting adventures. Gail does not really remember the haul, how much candy they got, but she does remember that delicious shiver of anticipation as she left the safety of a familiar home and stepped into an almost always white world of mystery and the unknown. You can imagine her surprise when she was in Australia and realized for the first time that Halloween is not a universal celebration. Several of the North Americans threw a Halloween party anyway which was well attended. The police were summoned by the neighbours who, not understanding the significance, were frightened by the costumes. After that she informed her neighbours of all her plans and "strange" customs well in advance!

A folk character who is not attached to any particular time of the year but plays an important role in the lives of our young children is the tooth fairy. The tooth fairy is a rather recent addition to the world of folklore, appearing in our homes only during this century and only included in the world of children's literature in the last few years. The modern version of the tooth fairy, according to the children we asked, is very close to the image of Disney's "Tinkerbell" from the film *Peter Pan*.

The loss of the first tooth is commemorated in diverse ways around the world and, in the west, we have extended that honour to all the baby teeth. It is a worry, of course, that the tooth fairy will not be aware of the lost tooth or the location of the child who lost it. Esther lost a tooth while the family was on holiday in the Netherlands. After much turmoil and discussion she placed her tooth under her pillow and was delighted the next morning to discover her parents were right: the tooth fairy knew where to find her, and even more exciting, left a Canadian dollar bill rather than a Dutch coin. When they returned home, Esther visited the dentist and found that a tooth had to be pulled to make room for a new arrival. She was worried the tooth fairy would not appear for pulled teeth and told the dentist what had happened on holidays and how the Dutch tooth fairy gave her a dollar instead of the usual quarter. He reassured her all would be fine and gave her two dollars because, he said, "a Dutch tooth fairy was not any better than a Canadian one."

And for those who are travelling the superhighway of computer technology, connect to the Internet discussions on urban folklore, also known as contemporary legends. This is a highly popular discussion group with high school and university students. *Urban folklore*, or *contemporary legends*, the stories we have heard as having really happened to a "friend-of-a-friend," show up in newspapers as actual news items, in advice columns written by Abby Van Buren and Ann Landers, and on the comics pages. They are the stories that are swapped by teenagers as well as adults whenever they meet or talk on the telephone.

Did you know that when the High Level bridge was being built in Edmonton one of the concrete pillars had an

*additional ingredient? Apparently, as my friend's uncle's
grandfather told the story, two of the construction workers
could not get along and one of them went missing the
morning the concrete was poured! He was never heard
from again.*

The person who told us this story wanted to know if it was true or
not, but the story is told about countless bridges and building
sites—a contemporary legend. The freshest legends are exchanged
and discussed on the network with the same frequency they are told
and discussed face-to-face. They are modern folktales, proof positive that folklore is not something old and forgotten but something
vital and living and totally relevant for us and our children. (An
exploration of contemporary legends, their functions in today's
society and their possible folkloric antecedents can be found in the
book *Tales, Rumors and Gossip* by Gail de Vos.)

Enterprising teachers have always known the value of providing
connections between the "real" world and the school for their
students. Folklore is a vital teaching tool that has long-lasting
results. Merle's sons are now grown men but they still remember
the lessons of one grade five teacher who taught one class a week
called "Pop Literature." Their teacher introduced them to ballads,
pop songs, poetry set to music, and hard rock. First, they listened to
the song a few times, then he handed out the lyrics and the discussion began. He told them every song was really a story in itself, and
the class would try to identify what lay behind the words. What was
the writer's frame of mind when composing the lyrics? Was there a
message or was it just pure expression? Was it an interpretation of
an old song or folktale?

*We had some great dinner conversations on "Pop Literature"
days; dusted off some old records, sang the songs from the
handouts, carried on the discussions started in the classroom. We listened to the boys' versions of the stories, what
they liked and disliked, how they interpreted the lyrics and
what the music said to them.*

There is much controversy about some of the lyrics in today's popular music; rather than ignoring or banning them, try discussing the lyrics. An important part of storytelling is listening, an often ignored skill. Listening is how we get new stories—maybe it's necessary to hear the stories our children are listening to, and to come to an understanding of why they need to hear them. What we listened to, and what our children are listening to are going to be part of the popular culture of the future. It is important to understand what messages we are leaving behind.

Think back to the music you listened to—see if there are some connections, some stories you can tell of your uncertainty or dissatisfaction with life back then. Most of us "baby boomers" have fond memories of the music of our teenage years and, as well, have stories of clashes with our parents over our choices (and volume levels). Merle remembers how intensely her mother disliked the Beatles, yet she knows her mother never really sat down and listened to a record. A lot of her mother's arguments about the Beatles came from what she read and heard. Merle herself can't claim to like or understand a lot of the music her sons played in the house over the years, but she always knew why they listened to it.

As parents we must be aware of the world our children inhabit. One major signpost of that world is the music they both listen to and watch in video format. We can learn a great deal about how hopeless many young people feel today just by "hearing" the stories they are listening to and singing.

The other technology using traditional literature for a base is computerized games. Some of these games are "quest" games rather than games of violence, and in most instances a knowledge of traditional tales, folk literature and specific epics, such as Homer's Iliad, is needed to advance from level to level. The questions are subtle and players who have some knowledge of story are better able to play through the various levels because they see similarities and parallels with the folklore. As Merle recalls, this was borne out many years ago in her household when these games were in their infancy.

> *One game had the boys and all their friends stumped at one level, the clue being "The Pirate said. . . ." In desperation, after weeks of trying, they turned to me. "Try 'Yo, ho, ho and a bottle of rum,' " I suggested. That was it and* Treasure Island *was rediscovered.*

In some cases, there is no subtlety, the stories are obviously copied from a traditional story. These imitations are especially noticeable with certain fantasy adventure games that closely echo myths and legends.

This quick survey of folklore in popular culture provides only a brief glimpse at what is surrounding us in all aspects of our daily lives. It can do no harm, and certainly a great deal of good, for both adults and children to become familiar with the most common tales and rhymes. Families who know the stories behind their reading and viewing pleasure, the meaning and intent of advertisers and merchants, and the delight of the use of the most appropriate word will have a much enriched life.

"This story really has no end. We can start it over and tell it again."

AFTERWORD

We have enjoyed reaching back into our memories as well as learning more about each other and the individual memories of our families. Although we already knew the power of story and the communication channels opened by telling stories in our families, writing this book crystallized them for us.

We hope that by dipping into our real-life stories and some of the suggested resources, you, too, will discover the joy and power of storytelling. Never forget the age old story beginning, *"Once upon a time. . . ."* Use also *"When I was your age . . ."* and *"When you were only three years old . . ."* with your children regardless of their age. Remember, too, the importance of stories from grandparents or relatives and, if they are far away, ask them to record their stories so your children can connect with their roots and get a sense of their heritage and identity.

This is one of the strongest gifts you can give because family stories, if remembered and told, will survive moves, shifts in fortune, hard times and chaotic times. And they will help the family, and the individuals who comprise it, to survive and flourish.

Thank you for accompanying us on our story journey—we know you will enjoy the journeys on which you embark.

STORYTELLING RESOURCES

Storytelling

A recent resurgence of interest in storytelling has resulted in a myriad of books addressing different aspects of telling stories—in schools, libraries and in the home. The following list includes both classic and newly published titles recommended for those who wish to delve deeper into the world of storytelling. Some are out-of-print and may only be found in your local library.

Baker, Augusta and Ellin Green. *Storytelling: Art & Technique.* 2nd Edition. New York: R.R. Bowker, 1987.
> An overview of storytelling in all its aspects (values of storytelling, finding, learning, and preparing stories) as well as telling stories to people with special needs. Emphasis on storytelling in the library environment.

Barton, Bob. *Tell Me Another: Storytelling and Reading Aloud at Home, in the School and in the Community.* Markham, Ont.: Pembroke, 1986. (Distributed in the USA by Heinemann Educational Books).
> Filled with advice, book lists and excellent ideas. Discusses story patterns, making the story your own and storytelling in the classroom. Explores reading stories aloud to children.

Barton, Bob and David Booth. *Stories in the Classroom: Storytelling, Reading Aloud and Roleplaying with Children*. Markham, Ont.: Pembroke, 1991.

> Not only applicable to telling stories in schools but a fountain of valuable information for parents and caregivers. Focuses on children telling tales in various formats: orally, written, dramatic and visually. Discussions on the power of story, the story tribe or community, and how to find and learn a story.

Bauer, Caroline Feller. *New Handbook for Storytellers: With Stories, Poems, Magic, and More*. Chicago, American Library Association, 1993.

> Filled with ideas, bibliographies and hints for storytelling and story-hours. Dips into sources of stories—written and non-narrative (including sign language), multimedia storytelling including magic and music, as well as programming for all ages.

Breneman, Lucille N. and Bren Breneman. *Once Upon a Time: A Storytelling Handbook*. Chicago: Nelson-Hall, 1983.

> Focuses on choosing the "right" story, and working for fluency, characterization, visualization, body action, and unity and control when telling stories. Includes an annotated bibliography of stories appropriate for telling.

Dailey, Sheila. *Putting the World in a Nutshell: The Art of the Formula Tale*. New York: H.W.Wilson, 1994.

> Developed for beginning storytellers. Dailey concentrates on nine classic types of tales that are simple to learn and tell. There are examples for each type (38 in all) as well as hints and suggestions for making the stories your own. Highly recommended!

de Vos, Gail. *Storytelling for Young Adults: Techniques and Treasury*. Littleton, Col.: Libraries Unlimited, 1991.

> Of interest to people working and living with teenagers, this book examines the rationale and values behind telling stories to this age group and includes an annotated bibliography of over 200 age-appropriate stories with a theme index of the stories.

de Vos, Gail. *Tales, Rumors, and Gossip: Exploring Contemporary Folk Literature in Grades 7 - 12*. Littleton, Col.: Libraries Unlimited, 1995.

> An exploration of the stories (often told as "true") and the themes that capture the imagination of young people today. After an overview and discussion of these contemporary legends (modern urban myths), Gail examines them in their relationship to rumors and gossip, ostension (acting out the legends), the role of the media in formulation and dissemination and related genres (e.g. literary horror stories).

de Wit, Dorothy. *Children's Faces Looking Up: Program Building for the Storyteller*. Chicago: American Library Association, 1979.

> Aimed at storytellers preparing a storytelling programme, de Wit offers information for the non-professional as well. Her discussions on recognizing the tellable tale and modifying stories are very valuable. Equally valuable are the numerous story suggestions and bibliography.

Lane, Marcia. *Picturing the Rose: A Way of Looking at Fairy Tales: A Discussion of the Nature and Meaning of Fairy Tales with Explanation of the Process for Preparing Seven Multicultural Tales for Telling*. New York: H.W.Wilson, 1994.

> "Intended for both beginning and accomplished storytellers who wish to tell fairy tales with confidence and authenticity." Essays on various aspects of fairy tales in the past and present as well as seven stories demonstrating various methods of preparing stories for learning. For serious students of the art of storytelling.

Livo, Norma J. and Sandra A. Rietz. *Storytelling: Process and Practice*. Littleton, Col.: Libraries Unlimited, 1986.

> Although this book covers all the essential ingredients for successful storytelling it is not for the casual reader. Delves into the function of storytelling, story structure, learning stories and working with audiences. Includes a vast reservoir of story resources and "nonstory" resources such as games and songs. Useful appendices round out the exploration of story and storytelling.

MacDonald, Margaret Read. *The Parent's Guide to Storytelling.* HarperCollins, 1995.

> A collection of easy-to-tell tales with how-to suggestions. MacDonald, a librarian and well respected storyteller, is a prolific writer on the art of storytelling.

MacDonald, Margaret Read. *The Storyteller's Start-Up Book.* Little Rock: August House, 1993.

> The subtitle on this useful book is "Finding, Learning, Performing and Using Folktales including Twelve Tellable Tales". Topics include an invitation to storytell, your place in tradition, the values of storytelling (for all ages) as well as learning, performing and teaching others the art of storytelling. Includes extensive bibliographies.

Maguire, Jack. *Creative Storytelling: Choosing, Inventing, and Sharing Tales for Children.* Cambridge, Mass.: Yellow Moon Press, 1985.

> A useful dialogue on the values and history of storytelling, the types of traditional stories, how to learn stories, and how to create your own.

The National Storytelling Association. *Tales as Tools: The Power of Story in the Classroom.* Jonesborough, Tenn.: National Storytelling Press, 1994.

> Although focused on teachers and librarians in the school environment, this book includes numerous articles of interest to the "general" practitioner of storytelling: helping children develop and maintain listening skills, using stories to teach about peace and the environment, and turning parents into tellers.

Pellowski, Anne. *The World of Storytelling: A Practical Guide to the Origins, Development, and Applications of Storytelling.* Revised Edition. Bronx, N.Y.: H.W.Wilson, 1990.

> A scholarly yet approachable treatment of storytelling which delves into the history of storytelling, types of storytelling around the world (bardic, religious, storytelling in the home, storyhours in libraries and playgrounds) as well as the format and style of storytelling.

Rosen, Betty. *And None of it was Nonsense: The Power of Storytelling in School*. Scholastic, 1988.

> Highly recommended. Captures the essence and values of telling stories to communicate to people of different cultures and backgrounds. Based on her experience in an inner-city London (England) boys school, Rosen describes how telling stories opened windows and doors to her students (8 to 18) who, at the start, did not share a common language or culture with any of their classmates.

Sawyer, Ruth. *The Way of the Storyteller: A great storyteller shares her rich experience and joy in her art, and tells eleven of her best-loved stories*. Penguin, 1970.

> The subtitle of the book says it all! Highly recommended. First published in 1942, Sawyer's book has been an inspiration to all of us interested in the art of storytelling.

Shedlock, Marie L. *The Art of the Storyteller*. New York: Dover, 1951. (Reprint of 1915 publication)

> A classic, but pertinent, personal discussion on the elements of learning a story. Topics include the difficulties of the story, the essentials of the story and elements to seek in the choice of material. Eighteen stories are also included in full text from the world of folklore and Hans Christian Andersen.

Stotter, Ruth. *About Story: Writings on Stories and Storytelling* 1980-1994. Stinson Beach, CA: Stotter Press, 1994.

> A collection of previously published articles. Includes the essentials for the understanding and learning of story dressed in elegant, but practical prose. Discussions include spirituality and storytelling, the storyteller as bridge between cultures and storytelling as a cooperative learning experience.

Yolen, Jane. *Touch Magic: Fantasy, Faerie and Folklore in the Literature of Childhood*. New York: Philomel, 1981.

> Does not focus on storytelling but on the entire realm of enriching children's lives with story and the ability to use imagination. Highly recommended.

Ziskind, Sylvia. *Telling Stories to Children.* New York: H.W.Wilson, 1976.

> Practical and easy to read and digest, Ziskind discusses story selection, learning the story and mastering techniques of telling stories. She also includes chapters on poetry, creative dramatics and planning the story hour for public libraries.

Family History

The titles included in this bibliography are all dedicated to gathering and telling the stories of the family. Several books analyze what impact these stories have had on family members.

Akeret, Dr. Robert U. *Family Tales, Family Wisdom: How to Gather the Stories of a Lifetime and Share Them with your Family*. New York: William Morrow, 1991.

> Highly recommended. Discussions on respecting elders of the community, discovering the hero in your life and using photographs and memories to bring the stories to light. Very readable.

Davis, Donald. *Telling Your Own Stories: For Family and Classroom Storytelling, Public Speaking, and Personal Journaling*. Little Rock: August House, 1993.

> A "how-to" handbook (that actually fits in the hand) addressing elements of story and story structure. Includes numerous memory "prompts" to elicit stories.

Greene, Bob and D.G. Fulford. *To Our Children's Children: Preserving Family Histories for Generations to Come*. New York: Doubleday, 1993.

> A series of questions to elicit stories from family members. The recommendations of these popular newspaper columnists (who just happen to be siblings) are sound for the most part.

However, their focus is on the writing or recording of the stories, usually in isolation from family members, to be given to their families at a later date. Recommended for the types of questions included in the book but take the time to tell the stories with your family.

Moore, Robin. *Awakening the Hidden Storyteller: How to Build a Storytelling Tradition in Your Family.* Boston: Shambala, 1991.
A guide for parents and children in creating, telling and listening to stories within the family.

Rosenbluth, Vera. *Keeping Family Stories Alive: A Creative Guide to Taping Your Family Life & Love.* Vancouver: Hartley & Marks, 1990.
Offers practical techniques for reviving and keeping family stories alive. Focuses on the process of gathering the tales and recording them on both audio and video equipment.

Stone, Elizabeth. *Black Sheep and Kissing Cousins: How Our Family Stories Shape Us.* New York: Penguin, 1988.
Perspective on the functions of family stories and their importance in our daily lives promoting family identities and individual aspirations. Recommended.

Stone, Richard. *Stories: The Family Legacy. A Guide for Recollection and Sharing.* Maitland, Fl.: StoryWork Institute Press, 1994.
This pamphlet covers a diverse number of topics about gathering and telling stories. The focus of the author is the collection of stories from the terminally ill to aid both the patient and the family members.

Zeitlin, Steven J., Amy J. Kotkin, and Holly Cutting Baker. *A Celebration of American Family Folklore: Tales and Traditions from the Smithsonian Collection.* Cambridge, MA: Yellow Moon, 1982.
A survey of American family folklore exploring the universal themes of family stories along with family sayings, family customs and family photographs. Includes a useful guide for collecting your own family folklore.

FAMILY STORIES: RECOMMENDED PICTURE BOOKS

This is just a sample of the many picture books, based on family stories, which are available. The books we have chosen to list show not only how story can be found in even the most mundane family event, but also how important it is to ensure that similar stories become part of your family's heirlooms.

Bogart, Jo Ellen. *Mama's Bed*. Richmond Hill: North Winds Press, 1993.
> Mama's bed is the best place to be—whether you are sad or happy. Wonderful story of a single parent family.

Bruchac, Joseph. *Fox Song*. Toronto: Oxford University Press, 1993.
> Jamie adores her grandmother, and when she dies, the little girl finds a way to help ease the pain.

Bunting, Eve. *Sunshine Home*. New York: Clarion, 1994.
> A little boy shows the way for a family to express their real feelings when his grandmother is in a nursing home recovering from a broken hip.

Bunting, Eve. *Wednesday Surprise*. New York: Clarion, 1989.
> Anna and grandma get together on Wednesday nights and read picture books out loud. They are preparing a surprise for dad's birthday gift.

Colbert, Jan. *Good Night*. Toronto: HarperCollins, 1993.
> With mum's help, everyday activities are not only fun, but hint of fantasy.

de Paolo, Tomi. *Tom*. New York: Putnam, 1993.
> Drawing on childhood memories, de Paolo tells a touching story about the relationship between Tom and his grandfather for whom he is named.

Eyvindson, Peter. *The Yesterday Stone*. Winnipeg: Pemmican, 1992.
> Story of a little girl's strong relationship with her grandmother and what she learns from it.

Farrell, Sue. *To the Post Office with Mama*. Willowdale, Annick, 1994.
> A two year old and mother go on a trip one cold winter day to mail a letter.

Ferber, Elizabeth. *Once I Was Very Small*. Willowdale, Annick, 1993.
> Using her photo album to jog her memory, a little girl introduces us to how she grew up .

Fernandes, Eugenie. *Just You and Me*. Willowdale, Annick, 1994.
> How mum and a little girl find some special time together after the new and demanding baby arrives!

Fox, Mem. *Sophie*. New York: Harcourt Brace, 1994.
> Simple and beautiful story of the love between a little girl and her grandfather and how that love is passed on.

Gilman, Phoebe. *Something From Nothing*. Richmond Hill: North Winds Press, 1992.
> A story, re-told from an old folk song, about the wisdom of a grandfather. (See Stanfield, Steve.)

Greenfield, Eloise. *Grandpa's Face*. New York: Philomel Books, 1988.
> How a little girl teaches her grandfather that sometimes his face can be scary.

Gregoy, Valiska. *Through the Mickle Woods*. Boston, Little, Brown and Company, 1992.
> After his wife's death, a grieving king follows her wishes and journeys with a small boy to a bear's cave in the mickle woods. There he hears three stories that allow him to once again appreciate the beauty of the world.

Henkes, Kevin. *Owen*. New York: Greenwillow Books, 1993.
> How everyone works to come up with a solution to help Owen "give up" his favourite blanket before he starts school.

Hoffman, Mary. *Amazing Grace*. London: Frances Lincoln, 1991.
> Heartwarming story about how a grandmother proves to a little girl that she "can be anything she sets her mind to."

Hoffman, Mary. *Grace's Family*. London: Frances Lincoln, 1995.
> Grace and her family visit her papa's compound in Gambia, Africa.

Lawson, Julie. *My Grandfather Loved the Stars*. Victoria: Beach Holme, 1992.
> A wonderful exploration of the relationship between a little girl and her grandfather and a combined interest in the stars.

Lindbergh, Reeve. *Grandfather's Lovesong*. New York: Viking, 1993.
> A grandfather shows his grandchild that his love is unconditional and never-ending.

Lottridge, Celia. *The Name of the Tree*. Toronto: Groundwood, 1989.
> This retelling of a Bantu legend revolves around the memory of story told by a great-great-great grandmother.

Mamchur, Carolyn with Meguido Zolo. *In the Garden*. Winnipeg: Pemmican, 1993.
> Joyce plants some seeds her grandmother left her and discovers the meaning of the forget-me-nots embroidered on a handkerchief. She takes up her grandmother's nurturing.

McDonald, Megan. *The Great Pumpkin Switch*. New York: Orchard, 1992.

> Grampa tells the story of how he and his best friend smash the pumpkin his sister had been growing for a competition.

Oberman, Sheldon. *The Always Prayer Shawl*. Honesdale, PA: Boyd Mills, 1993.

> A wonderfully warm story about family life and tradition.

Polacco, Patricia. *My Ol'Man*. New York: Philomel Books, 1995.

> Story of a very special father who teaches the importance of magic, hope and dreams.

Porte, Barbara Ann. *When Grandma Almost Fell off the Mountain & Other Stories*. New York: Orchard, 1993.

> Stella and Zelda's first request when they visit their grandmother is for a story. She tells them hilarious stories about a trip she and her sister took to Florida when they were their age.

Reynolds, Marilynn. *Belle's Journey*. Victoria: Orca, 1993.

> A little girl and her horse in a prairie blizzard, based on stories the author heard from her grandmother and mother.

Sanfield, Steve. *Bit by Bit*. New York: Philomel, 1995.

> An old song, wonderfully retold as a heartwarming story, proving that stories come from little events. (See also Gilman, Phoebe.)

Say, Allen. *Grandfather's Journey*. New York: Houghton Mifflin, 1993.

> The story of a Japanese-American's grandfather's journey to America and how the story effects him years later.

Shea, Pegi Deitz. *The Whispering Cloth: A Refugee's Story*. Honesdale, PA: Boyds Mill Press, 1995.

> A poignant tale about Mai, a Hmong refugee, who learns from her grandmother how to stitch a *pa'ndau* (a story cloth). A story about a young girl's hope in the midst of war in a refugee camp.

Vaage, Carol. *Bibi and the Bull*. Edmonton: Dragon Hill Publishing, 1995.

> A warm story about a warm and loving relationship between a grandfather and his spunky little granddaughter.

Weisman, Joan. *The Storyteller*. New York: Rizzoli, 1993.
> A little girl and an elderly neighbour share the stories which are important to them. The Pueblo storyteller doll is also introduced and explained.

Williams, Sophy. *Nana's Garden*. Mississauga: Random House, 1992.
> Thomas meets a little girl in his nana's garden who allows him to see his grandmother at his age.

Williams, David. *Grandma Essie's Covered Wagon*. New York: Knopf, 1993.
> A grandmother's story of her pioneer childhood—a great start to exploring our own family stories.

Yolen, Jane. *Owl Moon*. New York: Philomel, 1987.
> Memories of a family's special outing to find the owls.

Zolotow, C. *This Quiet Lady*. New York: HarperCollins, 1992.
> How family traditions are passed on to future generations, when a little girl tells her mother's history from family photographs.

RECOMMENDED STORY COLLECTIONS

The following list includes some of our favourite reading of all time. These books are written for the adult reader who can then take the tale and tell it in his or her own words for their children, spouses, parents or friends. Enjoy the journey to discover the types of tales you like best. {Basic Theme of Collection}

Abrahams, Roger D. *Afro-American Folktales: Stories from Black Traditions in the New World*. Panthcon Fairy Tale and Folklore Library, 1985.

Afanas'ev, Aleksandr. *Russian Fairy Tales*. Pantheon Fairy Tale and Folklore Library, 1945.

Barchers, Suzanne. *Wise Women: Folk and Fairy Tales from Around the World*. Littleton, Col: Libraries Unlimited, 1990. {Female protagonists}

Bjurstrom, C.G. *French Folktales from the Collection of Henri Pourrat*. Translated by Royall Tyler. Pantheon Fairy Tale and Folklore Library, 1989.

Calvino, Italo. *Italian Folktales*. Pantheon Fairy Tale and Folklore Library, 1980.

Carter, Angela. *The Old Wives' Fairy Tale Book.* Pantheon Fairy Tale and Folklore Library, 1990. (British edition: *The Virago Book of Fairy Tales*) {Female Protagonists}

Carter, Angela. *The Second Virago Book of Fairy Tales.* Virago, 1992. {Female Protagonists}

Chinen, Allan B. *Beyond the Hero: Classic Stories of Men in Search of Soul.* Jeremy P. Tarcher/Putnam, 1993. {Tales of masculinity}

Chinen, Allan B. *In the Ever After: Fairy Tales and the Second Half of Life.* Chiron, 1989. {Tales reflecting old age}

Chinen, Allan B. *Once Upon a Midlife: Classic Stories and Mythic Tales to Illuminate the Middle Years.* Jeremy P. Tarcher, 1992. {Middle-age Heroes}

Clarkson, Atelia and Gilbert B. Cross. *World Folktales.* Scribner's, 1980. {Multicultural}

Cole, Joanna. *Best-Loved Folktales.* Garden City, N.Y.: Doubleday, 1982. {Multicultural}

Courlander, Harold and George Herzog. *The Cow-Tail Switch and Other West African Stories.* New York: Henry Holt, 1947.

Crossley-Holland, Kevin. *Folk Tales of the British Isles.* Pantheon Fairy Tale and Folklore Library, 1985.

Erdoes, Richard and Alfonso Ortiz. *American Indian Myths and Legends.* Pantheon Fairy Tale and Folklore Library, 1984.

Goss, Linda and Marian E. Barnes. *Talk that Talk: An Anthology of African-American Storytelling.* Simon & Schuster, 1989.

Holt, David & Bill Mooney. *Ready-to-Tell Tales: Sure-Fire Stories from America's Favorite Storytellers.* Little Rock: August House, 1994. {Multicultural}

Kane, Alice. *The Dreamer Awakes.* Peterborough: Broadview Press, 1995. {Multicultural}

Kendall, Carol & Yao-wen Li. *Sweet and Sour: Tales from China*. New York: Clarion, 1978.

Lang, Andrew. *Blue Fairy Book*. Original published by Longmans, Green, 1889. {European}
> Other "colours" in this valuable series include: *Red Fairy Book, Green Fairy Book, Yellow Fairy Book, Violet Fairy Book, Olive Fairy Book, Lilac Fairy Book, Brown Fairy Book, Orange Fairy Book, Grey Fairy Book,* and *Crimson Fairy Book.* {Multicultural}

Livo, Norma J. and Dia Cha. *Folk Stories of the Hmong: Peoples of Laos, Thailand, and Vietnam*. Englewood, Col: Libraries Unlimited, 1991.

MacDonald, Margaret Read. *Look Back and See: Twenty Lively Tales for Gentle Tellers*. Bronx, N.Y.: H.W. Wilson, 1991. {Non-violent themes}

MacDonald, Margaret Read. *Twenty Tellable Tales: Audience Participation Folktales for the Beginning Storyteller*. Bronx, N.Y.: H.W. Wilson, 1986. {Multicultural}

MacDonald, Margaret Read. *When the Lights Go Out: Twenty Scary Tales to Tell*. Bronx, N.Y.: H.W. Wilson, 1988. {Halloween}

Mayo, Margaret. *The Book of Magical Tales*. Illustrated by Jane Ray. Toronto: Doubleday Canada, 1993. {Multicultural}

McNeil, Heather. *Hyena and the Moon: Stories to Tell from Kenya*. Englewood, Col.: Libraries Unlimited, 1994.

Minghella, Anthony. *Jim Henson's "The Storyteller."* New York: Alfred A. Knopf, 1991. {European}

Moss, Anita and Jon Stott. *The Family of Stories: An Anthology of Children's Literature*. New York: Holt, Rinehart & Winston, 1986. {Multicultural; extensive reading lists}

National Association for the Preservation and Perpetuation of Storytelling. *Best-Loved Stories Told at the National Storytelling Festival*. National Storytelling Press, 1991. {Traditional and family stories}

National Association for the Preservation and Perpetuation of Storytelling. *More Best-Loved Stories Told at the National Storytelling Festival*. National Storytelling Press, 1992. {Traditional and family stories}

Pellowski, Anne. *The Family Storytelling Handbook*. MacMillan, 1987. {Traditional and family stories}

Pellowski, Anne. *The Story Vine: A Source Book of Unusual and Easy-to-Tell Stories from Around the World*. MacMillan, 1984. {Multicultural}

Penton, Mary Helen and Jacqueline DiGennaro. *Images of a People: Tlinglit Myths and Legends*. Englewood, Col.: Libraries Unlimited, 1992.

Roberts, Moss. *Chinese Fairy Tales & Fantasies*. Pantheon Fairy Tale and Folklore Library, 1979.

Schram, Peninnah. *Jewish Stories One Generation Tells Another*. Northvale, N.J.: Jason Aronson, 1987.

Schwartz Howard and Barbara Rush. *The Diamond Tree: Jewish Tales from Around the World*. New York: HarperCollins, 1991. {For children}

Smith, Jimmy Neil. *Homespun*. Crown Publishers, 1988. {Stories from well known American Storytellers}

Sherman, Josepha. *Rachel the Clever and Other Jewish Folktales*. Little Rock, Ark: August House, 1993.

Tyler, Royall. *Japanese Tales*. Pantheon Fairy Tale and Folklore Library, 1987.

Vathanaprida, Supaporn. *Thai Tales: Folktales of Thailand*. Edited by Margaret Read MacDonald. Englewood, Col.: Libraries Unlimited, 1994.

Vigil, Angel. *The Corn Woman: Stories and Legends of the Hispanic Southwest*. Englewood, Col.: Libraries Unlimited, 1994.

Yashinsky, Dan. *Next Teller*. Ragweed, 1993. {Stories from well known Canadian Storytellers}

Yashinsky, Dan. *Tales for an Unknown City: Stories from One Thousand and One Friday Nights of Storytelling.* McGill-Queen's University Press, 1990. {Stories told in Toronto at their weekly storytelling evening}

Yeats, W.B. *Fairy & Folk Tales of Ireland.* MacMillan, 1973.

Yee, Paul. *Tales from Gold Mountain: Stories of the Chinese in the New World.* Illustrated by Simon Ng. Vancouver: Groundwood, 1989. {Chinese-Canadian}

Yep, Laurence. *The Rainbow People.* Illustrated by David Wiesner. New York: Harper & Row, 1989. {Chinese-American}

Yolen, Jane. *Favorite Folktales from Around the World.* Pantheon Fairy Tale and Folklore Library, 1986. {Multicultural and highly recommended}

Young, Richard and Judy Dockrey Young. *African-American Folktales for Young Readers: Including Favorite Stories from Popular African and African-American Storytellers.* Little Rock, Ark.: August House, 1993.

Zipes, Jack. *Beauties, Beasts and Enchantment: Classic French Fairy Tales.* New York: New American Library, 1989.

Zipes, Jack. *The Complete Fairy Tales of the Brothers Grimm.* New York: Bantam, 1987.

Books Mentioned in Text

These stories are mentioned in our discussions on storytelling and appear in the same order in this list as they do in the book.

The Golem, a powerful Jewish legend, appears in many printed variations. Three suggested titles are:

> McDermott, Beverly Brodsky. *The Golem: A Jewish Legend.* J.B. Lippincott, 1976. (Picture book)

> Rosen, Michael. *The Golem of Old Prague.* Illustrated by Val Biro. Andre Deutsch, 1990.

> Singer, Isaac Bashevis. *The Golem.* Illustrated by Uri Shulevitz. Farrar-Straus-Giroux, 1982.

The Hanukkah of Great-Uncle Otto. Myron Levoy. The Jewish Publication Society of America, 1984.

Caps for Sale. Esphyr Slobodkina. W. R. Scott, 1947.

The True Story of the Three Little Pigs. Jon Scieszka. Viking, 1989.

We're Going On A Bear Hunt. Michael Rosen. Walker Brothers, 1993.

Ten Small Tales. Celia Barker Lottridge. Groundwood, 1993.

The Fat Cat. Jack Kent. Parents, 1971.

The Three and Many Wishes of Jason Reid. Hazel J. Hutchins. Annick Press, 1983.

Frank and Zelda. Maryann Kovalski. Kids Can Press, 1990.

The Magic Hockey Skates. Alan Morgan. Oxford University Press, 1991.

The Stinky Cheeseman and Other Fairly Stupid Stories. Jon Scieszka. Viking, 1992.

Somebody and the Three Blairs. Marilyn Tolhurst. Orchard, 1990.

Treasure Island. Robert Lewis Stevenson. 1911. (Numerous editions available)

UNIVERSAL TALES:
NURSERY RHYMES AND LULLABIES

Nursery rhyme collections are often chosen for their illustrations, and personal preferences play an important part. In some cases, however, it is the collection of rhymes that is important.

Crane, Walter. *Traditional Nursery Rhymes*. Kansas City: Andrews and McMeel, 1995. (Facsimile edition of undated publication originally titled *Baby's Opera*.)

de Paolo, Tomi, selected by. *Tomi de Paolo's Mother Goose*. New York: Putnam, 1985.

Emerson, Sally. *Baby Games and Lullabies*. New York: Kingfisher, 1993.

Engvick, William, ed. *Lullabies and Night Songs*. New York: HarperCollins, 1965.

Gilbert, Yvonne. *Baby's Book of Lullabies*. Newmarket: McClelland & Stewart, 1990.

Gill, Shelley. *The Alaska Mother Goose and Other North Country Nursery Rhymes*. Paws IV, 1987.

Kane, Sean. *Nursery Rhymes for Colicky Parents*. Scarborough: HarperCollins, 1995.

Lee, Dennis. *Jelly Belly*. Toronto: Macmillan, 1985.

Lee, Dennis. *Alligator Pie*. Toronto: Macmillan, 1974.

Lines, Kathleen. *Lavendar's Blue*. London: Oxford University Press, 1990.

Lobel, Arnold, selected by. *Random House Book of Mother Goose*. New York: Random House, 1986.

Lottridge, Celia Barker, selected by. *Mother Goose: A Canadian Sampler*. Toronto: Groundwood, 1994.

Lottridge, Celia Barker, selected by. *The Moon Is Round and Other Rhymes to Play With Your Baby*. Toronto: Parent-Child Mother Goose Program, 1992.

Masterson, Elizabeth, selected by. *This Little Puffin . . . Nursery Songs and Rhymes*. Harmondsworth: Puffin Books, 1969.

Mother Goose Nursery Rhymes Illustrated by Arthur Rackham. London: William Heineman, 1994. (Facsimile edition of 1913 publication.)

Opie, Iona and Peter Opie. *Tail Feathers From Mother Goose*. London: Walker Books, 1988.

Opie, Iona and Peter Opie. *The Puffin Book of Nursery Rhymes*. Harmondsworth: Puffin Books, 1963.

Opie, Iona and Peter Opie. *The Oxford Nursery Rhyme Book*. London: Oxford University Press, 1957.

Reid, Barbara. *Sing a Song of Mother Goose*. Richmond Hill: Scholastic, 1987.

Sharon, Lois & Bram's Mother Goose: Songs, Finger Rhymes, Tickling Verses, Games and More. Boston: The Atlantic Monthly Press, 1985.

Yolen, Jane, ed. *Lullaby Song Book*. New York: Harcourt Brace Jovanovich.

UNIVERSAL TALES:
COLLECTIONS OF MYTHS AND LEGENDS

Bach, Alice and J. Cheryl Exum. *Miriam's Well: Stories about Women in the Bible*. New York: Delcorte Press, 1991.
> A retelling of Old Testament stories focusing on women.

Bach, Alice and J. Cheryl Exum. *Moses' Ark: Stories from the Bible*. New York: Delcorte Press, 1989.
> A retelling of Old Testament stories.

Baltuck, Naomi. *Crazy Gibberish and Other Story Hour Stretches (from a storyteller's bag of tricks)*. Hamden, Conn.: Linnet Books, 1993.
> Includes songs, chants, riddles, tongue twisters and stories for the very young and their older siblings.

Clark, Ella Elizabeth. *Indian Legends of Canada*. Toronto: McClelland and Stewart, 1992. [Reprint of 1960 edition]
> A classic collection of tales native to Canada.

Connolly, Peter. *Greek Legends: The Stories, The Evidence*. New York: Simon & Schuster, 1993.
> A fascinating voyage into the Greek myths and research into the historical and artistic evidence of these tales. Aimed at young readers.

D'Aularie's, Ingri and Edgar Parin D'Aularie's. *D'Aularie's Book of Greek Myths*. New York: Doubleday, 1962.
> A popular collection for children, found in most public and school library collections.

D'Aularie's, Ingri and Edgar Parin D'Aularie's. *D'Aularie's Norse Gods and Giants*. New York: Doubleday, 1967.
> Retellings of the mythology of the Norsemen.

Dickson, Peter. *City of Gold and Other Stories From the Old Testament*. Illustrated by Michael Foreman. New York: Pantheon Books, 1980.
> Stories retold as they might have been from witnesses and family members, educated Egyptian priests, nomadic traders, and professional storytellers of the time.

Fowke, Edith. *Folktales of Canada*. Toronto: McClelland and Stewart, 1976.
> Includes both traditional and modern tales told by Canadians throughout history.

Fowke, Edith. *Folktales of French Canada*. Toronto: NC Press, 1979.
> Tall tales, folktales and other stories collected in Quebec.

Hamilton, Virginia. *In the Beginning: Creation Stories from Around the World*. Illustrated by Barry Moser. San Diego: Harcourt Brace Jovanovich, 1988.
> A superb collection of twenty-five myths from various cultures explaining the creation of the world.

Lottridge, Celia Barker and Alison Dickie. *Mythic Voices*. Scarborough: Nelson, 1991.
> Originally a school text book, this collection of myths from around the world is now available to everyone. A treasure trove.

Low, Alice. *The Macmillan Book of Greek Gods and Heroes*. Illustrated by Arvis Stewart. New York: Macmillan, 1994.
> A well researched and illustrated collection for all ages.

Norman, Howard. *Northern Tales: Traditional Stories of Eskimo and Indian Peoples*. Pantheon Fairy Tale and Folklore Library, 1990.
Traditional tales of the native tribes of the arctic and subarctic regions. Includes several regional maps and an explanation for the use of the word "Eskimo."

Rosen, Michael. *How the Animals Got Their Colors: Animal Myths from Around the World*. Toronto: Lester, 1992.
Colourful collection of tales enjoyed by all ages.

Saxby, Maurice and Robert Ingpen. *The Great Deeds of Heroic Women*. New York: Peter Bedrick, 1992.
A collection of tales relating the deeds of heroic female figures throughout the ages.

Saxby, Maurice and Robert Ingpen. *The Great Deeds of Superheroes*. New York: Peter Bedrick, 1989.
A collection of tales relating the deeds of heroic male figures throughout the ages.

Sutcliff, Rosemary. *Black Ships Before Troy: The Story of THE ILIAD*. Illustrated by Alan Lee. Toronto: Lester, 1993.
Very powerful retelling of this ancient story.

Zhang, Song Nan. *Five Heavenly Emperors: Chinese Myths of Creation*. Montreal: Tundra, 1994.
Powerful text and beautifully illustrated.

Universal Tales:
Traditional Tales Re-Told With a Twist

These titles, found either in the 398.2 or Picture Book sections, are listed under their traditional folktale title.

The Bremen Town Musicians

Kent, Jack. *The Bremen Town Musicians*. New York: Scholastic, 1974.

Page, P.K. *The Travelling Musicians*. Toronto: Kids Can Press, 1991.

Shute, Linda. *Momotaro the Peach Boy*. New York: Lothrop, Lee & Shepherd, 1986.

Cinderella

Cole, Babette. *Prince Cinders*. London: Collin Picture Lions, 1989.

Galdone, Paul. *Cinderella*. New York: McGraw Hill, 1978.

Greaves, Margaret. *Tattercoats*. New York: Random House, 1990.

Hooks, William H. *Moss Gown*. New York: Clarion Books, 1987.

Huck, Charlotte. *Princess Furball*. New York: Greenwillow, 1989.

Louie, Ai-Ling. *Yeh-Shen*. New York: Philomel, 1982.

Perrault, Charles. *Cinderella, or The Little Glass Slipper*. Harmondsworth, U.K.: Puffin, 1974.

Steptoe, John. *Mufaro's Beautiful Daughters*. New York: Lothrop, Lee & Shepard, 1987.

THE EMPEROR'S NEW CLOTHES

Adams, Michael. *The Emperor's New Clothes*. New Jersey: Unicorn Publishing, 1989.

Calmenson, Stephanie. *The Principal's New Clothes*. New York: Scholastic, 1989.

Mendelson, S.T. *The Emperor's New Clothes*. New York: Stewart Tabori & Chad, 1992.

Stevens, Janet. *The Emperor's New Clothes*. New York: Holiday House, 1985.

THE FROG PRINCE

Berenzy, Alix. *A Frog Prince*. New York: Henry Holt & Co., 1989.

Isadora, Rachel. *The Princess and the Frog*. New York: Greenwillow, 1989.

Sciezska, Jon. *The Frog Prince Continued*. New York: Viking, 1991.

GOLDILOCKS AND THE THREE BEARS

Brett, Jan. *Goldilocks and the Three Bears*. New York: G.P. Putnam's Sons, 1987.

Langley, Jonathan. *Goldilocks and the Three Bears*. New York: Harper Collins, 1992.

Marshall, James. *Goldilocks and the Three Bears*. New York: Dial, 1988.

Muir, Frank. *Goldilocks and the Three Bears*. London: Conran Octopus, 1992.

Turkle, Brinton. *Deep in the Forest*. New York: E.P. Dutton & Co. Inc., 1976.

HANSEL AND GRETEL
(By illustrator)

Adams, Adrienne. New York: Charles Scribner's Sons, 1975.

Browne, Antony. New York: Alfred A. Knopf, 1988.

Jeffers, Susan. New York: Dial Press, 1980.

Lesser, Rika. New York: G.P. Putnam's Sons, 1985.

Ross, Tony. London: Red Fox, 1991.

Wallace, Ian. Toronto: Groundwood, 1994.

Zwerger, Lisbeth. New York: Scholastic, 1991.

JACK AND THE BEANSTALK

Anolt, Catherine and Laurence. *Come Back Jack!* Cambridge, MS: Candlewick Press, 1994.

Biro, Val. *Jack and the Beanstalk*. Toronto: Oxford University Press, 1989.

Briggs, Raymond. *Jim and the Beanstalk*. London: Cavard, 1980.

Cole, Brock. *The Giant's Toe*. New York: Farrar, Straus & Giroux, 1987.

Garner, Allan. *Jack and the Beanstalk*. New York: Doubleday, 1992.

Kellog, Stephen. *Jack and the Beanstalk*. New York: Morrow, 1991.

Pearson, Susan. *Jack and the Beanstalk*. New York: Simon & Schuster, 1989.

Ross, Tony. *Lazy Jack*. New York: Dial, 1992.

Little Red Riding Hood

Coady, Christopher. *Little Red Riding Hood*. New York: Dutton Children's Books, 1991.

de Regniers, Beatrice Schenk. *Little Red Riding Hood*. New York: Aladdin Books, 1972.

Edens, Cooper. *Little Red Riding Hood*. New York: Simon Schuster, 1991.

Emberley, Michael. *Ruby*. Toronto: Little, Brown & Co., 1990.

Young, Ed. *Lon Po Po*. New York: Philomel, 1989.

Sleeping Beauty

Hyman, Trina Schart. *Sleeping Beauty*. Boston: Little, Brown & Co., 1977.

Thorn Rose. Middlesex: Puffin Books, 1977.

Yolen, Jane. *Sleeping Beauty*. New York: Ariel Books, 1989.

Yolen, Jane. *Sleeping Ugly*. New York: Coward, McCann & Geoghegan Inc., 1981.

Snow White

French, Fiona. *Snow White in New York*. New York: Oxford University Press, 1986.

The Three Little Pigs

Biro, Val. *The Three Little Pigs*. Toronto: Oxford University Press, 1990.

Celsi, Teresa. *The Fourth Little Pig*. Austin, Texas: Raintree Steck-Vaughn, 1994.

Hooks, William H. *The Three Pigs and the Fox*. New York: Macmillan, 1989.

Muir, Frank. *The Three Little Pigs*. London: Conran Octopus, 1993.

Offen, Hilda. *Nice Work, Little Wolf!* London: Puffin Books, 1992.

Trivizas, Eugene. *The Three Little Wolves and the Big Bad Pig*. London: Heinemann, 1993.

Zemach, Margot. *The Three Little Pigs*. New York: Farrar, Straus & Giroux, 1988.

TOM THUMB

Brenner, Barbara. *Little One Inch*. New York: Coward, McCann & Geoghegan, 1977.

Hughes, Monica. *Little Fingerling*. Toronto: Kids Can Press, 1989.

Morimoto, Junko. *The Inch Boy*. New York: Puffin Books, 1988.

Watson, Richard Jess. *Tom Thumb*. New York: Harcourt Brace Jovanich, 1989.

MISCELLANEOUS

Ada, Alma Flor. *Dear Peter Rabbit*. New York: Atheneum, 1994.

Geras, Adele. *My Grandmother's Stories*. London: Heinemann, 1990.

King-Smith, Dick. *The Topsy-Turvy Storybook*. London: Gollancz, 1992.

Little, Jean and Maggie de Vries. *Once Upon A Golden Apple*. Markham: Viking, 1991.

Rosen, Michael. *Hairy Tales and Nursery Crimes*. London: Young Lions, 1985.

Storytelling Organizations
and Other Resources

Storytelling organizations and newsletters abound. The resources given here will be able to give information about local groups and other publications.

T.A.L.E.S. (The Alberta League Encouraging Storytelling)
c/o WordWorks
2nd Floor, Percy Page Centre
11759 Groat Road
Edmonton, Alberta
T5M 3K6

The Storytellers School of Toronto
412-A College Street
Toronto, Ontario
M5T 1T3

National Storytelling Association
P.O. Box 309
Jonesborough, Tenn. 37659

Storytellers of Canada / Raconteur du Canada
c/o Rosalyn Cohen
2895 Hill Park Circle
Montreal, Quebec
H3H 1S8

The Parent-Child Mother Goose Program
107 Bathurst Street
Toronto, Ontario
M5R 3G8

Canadian Storytelling Directory
The Vancouver Society of Storytellers
4629 West 2nd Avenue
Vancouver, British Columbia
V6R 1L2

A Storyteller's Calendar
Stotter Press
P.O. Box 726
Stinson Beach, CA 94970

ABOUT THE AUTHORS

Telling Tales is the second book by award-winning Edmonton author and storyteller **Gail de Vos**. She is actively involved with T.A.L.E.S. (The Alberta League Encouraging Storytelling), Storytellers of Canada/Raconteur du Canada, and the National Storytelling Association. Besides telling stories and conducting workshops across Canada and in the United States, Gail teaches storytelling as well  as Canadian Children's Literature at the University of Alberta and is a resident storyteller at Fort Edmonton Historical Park. Gail and Merle are co-organizers of the Annual T.A.L.E.S./Fort Edmonton Park Storytelling Festival held each Labour Day weekend.

Telling Tales is the first book by Edmonton author and storyteller **Merle Harris**. Merle is a member of T.A.L.E.S., Storytellers of Canada/Raconteur du Canada and the National Storytelling Association. She used storytelling extensively while an elementary school library technician. Merle is a storyteller at Fort Edmonton Historical Park and facilitates the Parent–Child Mother Goose Programme  (which focuses on the joy and power of using nursery rhymes and stories together). She is also on the editorial staff of *Children's Book News*, published for the Canadian Children's Book Centre.